Three Mountains and a Voice

Three Mountains and a Voice

Reverend Wanda C. Outlaw

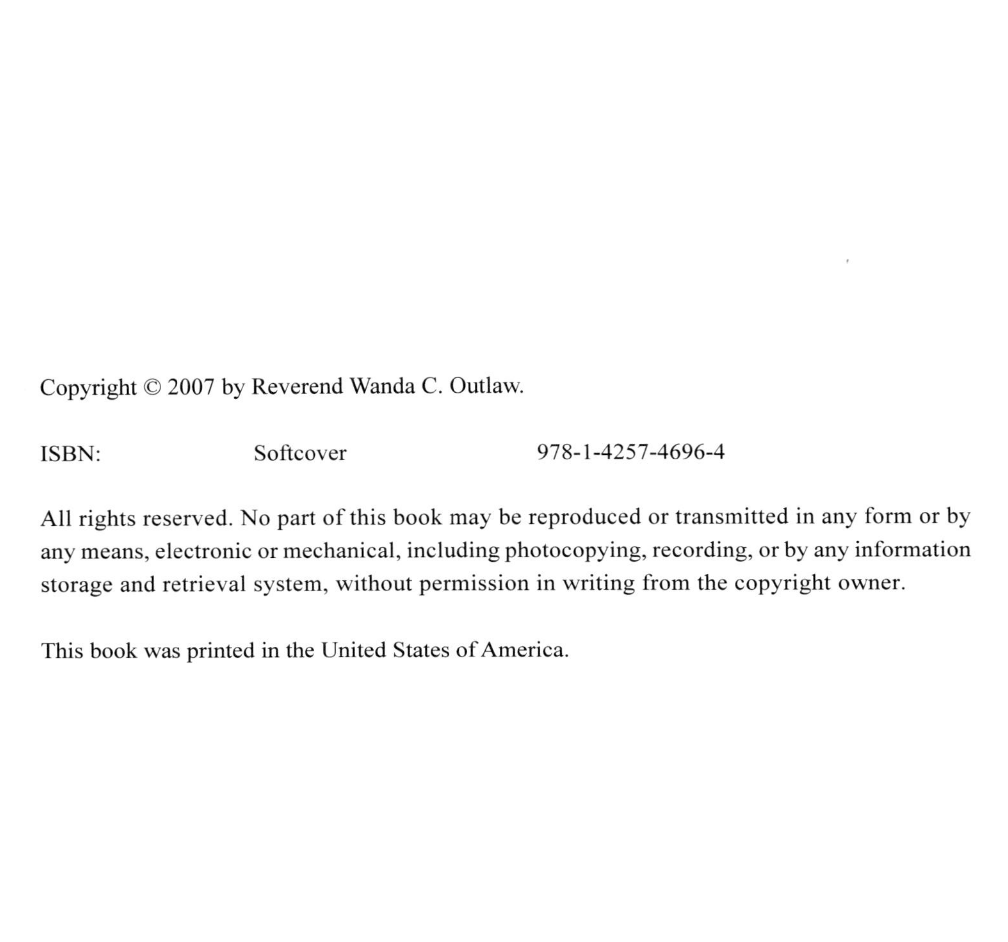

ISBN: Softcover 978-1-4257-4696-4

This book was printed in the United States of America.

To order additional copies of this book, contact:
Xlibris Corporation
1-888-795-4274
www.Xlibris.com
Orders@Xlibris.com

38075

Contents

Introduction 9
In The Genesis 13
The Making of A Revolutionary 17
A Writer's Soul 23
Lost In Man 27
Breakthrough 31
God Uses The Government 35
Only A Spirit Can Embrace Spirits 40
Transformation 44
A Little Voice 50
Seattle Makes Three 53
Motivators, Inspirationalists, and Teachers:
You Have My Undying Love 58
Denomination Did Not Call You 60
Today, If You Hear His Voice 63

First and foremost
The God of my Ancestors
Then
He who has been my strength, my teacher, my joy
From the womb until forever
My son
Stephen T. Outlaw, Jr.

Introduction

"When I grow up I want to be a police officer." "When I grow up I want to be a fireman." "I want to be a lawyer." Children want to be someone people look up to. How many children, specifically girls, say, "When I grow up I want to be a priest?" I didn't! But that is what happened in the midst of mountains in my life between adolescence and adulthood.

Mountains, high and low peaks, narrow cliffs, old tall trees that from afar look like plush ground cover, and sometimes the snow caps melt under the strength of the sun and give way to trickling waters that flow over various shapes and sizes of massive rock and dirt . . . these are our majestic mountains. Mountains, from Kilamanjaro to the Rockies, all shapes and sizes, they were created as backdrops to enhance the land to beautify the skies, and to motivate man/woman to overcome life's monumental obstacles.

From childhood to my adult years, my life can be described as majestic mountains. I had highs and lows, I periodically had, and still have, cliffs that I look over and wonder should I stay on the cliff or dive off but then it was sometimes hard to get a clear view, my direction was obscured because of all the tall trees. I often ran into snow that melted right from under my feet causing me to flow down between and over the rocky and dirty terrain of life. I am not talking about mountain climbing, that's not my thing. I am talking about life's peaks and slopes, highs and lows, the good times and the bad. The situations and people that I met along the way that made me want to hollar. I am also talking about the call to ordained ministry. I faced not one mountain, but three mountains and a voice!

This is my "Call" story. My Call to ordained ministry. *What makes this so special?* I am a Priest. I am also an African-American woman. At this point some people will close this book and put it back on the store bookshelf, I understand, it was hard for me to take at first. Now, at 52 years of age I understand that it is not about what man or what woman think, the Call is a personal, mountainous and monumental moment between the one Called and God.

I am sharing my Call to ordained ministry with everyone but especially women. So often women allow what society says is comfortable and right to dictate their destiny. God dictates your destiny and I feel better handling the mountain moments with God than with hu-man. Women and men have to follow the legal edicts of man, you know, give Caesar what is due Caesar, but you first, give God what is due God. **If you believe**, I mean really believe, in the power of the Almighty, then you know that God rules and reigns in your life, whether you be male or female.

I belong to a denomination that freed itself from the Roman Catholic Church in order to empower its people to take ownership and control over their own destiny moved by the genius of their culture. My denomination is The African-American Catholic Congregation (AACC); (the church is called Imani Temple), which is now 17 years old and still striving to the glory of God. The good people of the AACC have seen mountains, they have experienced that rough terrain, they have found out that it is not easy to start a church it requires hard work, consistency, much patience, and love. I learned the reverence and discipline of religion from the Roman Catholic Church but I opened up to the power of a wonder-working God through my parents and the AACC's Imani Temple. No matter what denomination you belong to you should be learning more and more about God and what God expects of you in your everyday living.

A student from Trinity College asked me an interesting question when I appeared as a speaker for a Feminist Theology class. *"What would you think about your denomination merging back with the Roman Catholic Church?"* Now, I know that you do not answer a question with a question but I could not resist. *"What do you think that would mean to me?"* Another student responded, *"You would not be a Priest any longer."* So very true at least in the mind of man. I have been ordained under the order of Melchezedek, so once a Priest always a Priest! Either God's word is Truth or it is not. I have come to find out that it is not about denomination building but Kingdom building. Yes, God gave man (woman) the genius to develop denominations so that everyone had a place of worship—a place where they could reach God in their understanding. But let's face it ministry is not inside four walls it is out in the streets. It is inside of every man and woman who takes charge of spreading the Good News.

I love all my clergy brothers and sisters and they have all taught me something about God, denomination building, administration, and direction.

Everyone comes with his or her own unique gifts. *"There are different kinds of spiritual gifts but the same Spirit; there are different forms of service but the same Lord; there are different workings but the same God who produces all of them in everyone." (1 Corinthians 12:4-6)*

My Call story keeps returning to the forefront of my mind for two reasons: 1) To remind me of who is in charge of my ministry . . . the One who Called me and 2) To share my journey with women (and men) who are not sure if they have been called especially if they have led a risqué life. In other words, I GOT A TESTIMONY! Jesus used Peter who denied him three times, he used Thomas (Didymus) who doubted him, and Jesus used Mary Magdala to preach the Good News of his resurrection. Now, if women were not to speak out, do you think Jesus would have used us to teach and spread his Father's word?!

"In the year A.D. 55 near the end of Paul's 3-year ministry in Ephesus the Corinthian culture did not allow women to confront men in public worship but they could at home. Paul's words were meant to promote unity." (NIV Study Application Bible Reference) As scholars of theology it is important to study to show thyself approved. If Paul did not support women speaking up **AT ALL** about the glory of God then he would not have had sisters in the gap who were to be treated as he was treated. In the Acts of the Apostles Paul spoke about the women who were in the vineyard . . . . The Diakonos . . . Phoebe (Deacon), Prisca, Aquila, and Mary, (Ministers), Junia (an Apostle), thought to be a man, was in actuality a woman. Now, if this does not help you or change your mind, then think about this. "*Then God Said: 'Let us make man in our image after our likeness.'" (Genesis 1:6 NAB) "God created man in his image, in the divine image he created him;* ***male and female*** *he created them." (Genesis 1:27 NAB)* It is time for us to embrace all that comes with this Scripture and stop limiting our thoughts as well as our living!

I want to dispense with the naysayers, the fear talkers, and the underpowered doubters right up front so that I can deal with the "meat and potato's" of my "Call" story. I do not begin to believe that I can still everyone's spirit about the Call of a woman especially to the Priesthood, but this book is for someone whom God is making ready to say, "Here I am Lord, send me!"

Let's Pray . . .

Holy and Wondrous God, God, who can do all things, God who has created all things, and who calls man and woman as His own to do His Holy work, we praise you God! We glorify and magnify all that you are to us and for us! God you who are both, Mother and Father to us bless us with wisdom and discernment as we follow just one woman's story. Lord I pray you stir the consciousness of the writer and the reader in Jesus Name. Amen.

In The Genesis

I was born and raised in Washington, D.C. I was raised in a two-parent household. My parents were raised in the "country," the rural areas. Cities south of D.C. are considered country. Mary Lena (Booze) Brown, my mom, was born in Bowie, Maryland when it was still woodsy and you had to travel dirt roads to reach the nearest house or trailer. Augustus King Brown, my dad, was born in Huntersville, North Carolina.

Washington, DC was filled with people who migrated from the deeper south, i.e., North Carolina, South Carolina, Georgia, or Alabama to seek a better life. My mom was a maid and my dad worked for the Post Office when it was under the federal government. Dad always encouraged me to work for the government because at that time in the 70's it was a secure job with leave and benefits. He wanted me to go to college, learn languages, and work at the State Department so that I could travel around the world to see and learn as much as possible.

I was also raised in a dual denominational household. My father was a Baptist, he never went to church but he knew Scriptures thanks to his sister who raised him. Mom was a devout Roman Catholic, in church every Sunday. I mean every Sunday unless she was deathly ill and I cannot ever remember mom ever being sick. If mom went to church, I went to church every Sunday, every feast day, and any special Masses or events. I made my First Holy Communion and Confirmation, so if you are Roman Catholic then you know I was inundated with the Baltimore Catechism followed by Catholic Christian Doctrine (CCD) Classes.

Let me tell you when my dad went to church. He went for my First Holy Communion ceremony where we also celebrated/coroneted the Blessed Virgin Mary, the Mother of Jesus. A statue of Mary was carried in a processional. There was dad with his Brownie Camera taking his little girls picture. Then Dad came to my Confirmation ceremony, where the candidates were quizzed by the Archbishop on questions that the nuns grilled and grilled us on over a period of weeks; questions that I today cannot remember. Confirmation is a Catholic rites of passage ceremony where the child becomes a young adult. In the Jewish faith it would be called a Bar mitzvah. I approached the Archbishop with a 3x5 card that had my Saint's name on it, "Cecelia" . . . Oh wait! The nuns said that my mom spelled it incorrectly, it should have been spelled "Cecilia." I don't think God cared so much about the spelling but more about whether I understood the story behind the person. Saint Cecelia took a vow of chastity but she was to marry a nobleman. She prayed to God to protect her virginity even in marriage. Her husband to be, after hearing of her vow to God, was willing to take her as his wife without forcing her to break her vow to God. She converted her husband and his brother to Christianity. Cecilia sang to God in her heart and is known as the Patron Saint of Music. Before her death it is said that she converted souls to Christianity even on her deathbed and she turned her home into a church.

I approached the archbishop, who looked kingly in his miter and robes, handed him my Saint's name, he said some "sacred" words calling me Cecelia and then he gave me a light slap on my cheek. I was already scared and then I was slapped out of it. I remember my father not being too crazy about his little girl being slapped by an old white man.

Dad's next trip to church that I knew of was to attend my cousin's funeral, a Baptist funeral. My Aunt Lexi (I called her Aunt rather than Cousin out of respect for her age) was active and well known in many Baptist Churches around the area. This was the first time I heard Gospel music. It reminded me of rock and roll except the choir was singing about Jesus and his goodness. My favorite song was "Traveling Shoes." I have never heard it sung the same way since. This was also the first time I experienced "the shout," not internally, but outwardly. I was sitting up straight next to my daddy on these soft cushioned pews. I was wearing my black patent leather Mary Jane shoes and white frilly socks. I had on my tan straw hat, you know the one, it had a brim trimmed in white silk ribbon with a bow on the back that extended down my back. Suddenly, out of know where, this lady jumped up and as she threw her hands up she knocked my bonnet down over my eyes. I turned around and looked at her with my mouth open wide. I asked my dad, "Daddy, why did that lady hit me?" Dad nicknamed me Poopee . . . "Poopee, she got happy." She was screaming and jumping until she fell out in the pew while another lady was lapping the church aisles as others were screaming. They loved the song as much as I did! "Daddy, I don't hit people when I'm happy and why is that lady running indoors?" Dad, with a chuckle, told me to turn around and he said that she did not mean it. I thought that going to church whether Catholic or Baptist could be quite dangerous especially this shout thing.

The last time dad went to church was for my wedding. It was the latter part of July and it was hot. Dad had trouble breathing in the heat. We were grateful that the church had air conditioning. I gave the Priest a fit about how I wanted my ceremony to go. The Priest wanted a Mass and I did not want a Mass I wanted it to be quick and done. The Priest continued telling us how it should be and I kept telling him how I wanted it. Dad intervened told me to "cool-out" and relax, so I did what Daddies little girls do, I folded my arms, pouted, and I got my way. My dad was able to walk his little girl down the aisle in peace and comfort. It is amazing what people will tolerate for love. My dad did not fight the Roman edict that if one parent is Roman Catholic then the children must be raised Roman Catholic. He did not fight it because he was not attending church anywhere and it was important to him that I have some form of religious education. The Bible said raise up a child in the way they should go and they shall not depart from it. I am living proof of this.

My parents raised a quiet little girl. I did not talk much. My dad said that you could learn more with your mouth closed rather than talking all the time. He was right. I played with my dolls, which were white and black. I never thought about people being different colors until one day I was rocking in my rocking chair watching our black and white television and the President of the United States Eisenhower was speaking. I stared at this man and then I looked at the back of my hands. I looked at Eisenhower then looked at my hands. My dad was sitting behind me in his favorite brown chair by the window, smoking his pipe filled with Holiday Tobacco, watching me, and taking note of my observations.

"Daddy, who is he?"

"The President of the United States, President Eisenhower."

"Daddy, why is he a different color from me?"

My father let out a groan . . .

"Poopie, he is white and we are colo . . . we are black."

My dad was one of the few adults who used the term black in the 60's. His generation thought that the term "black" when speaking of a person's race was an insult—a slander. The mind-set of that time was that black was ugly or negative . . . we were Colored. I thought about what he told me for only a moment and continued to rock in my chair.

Dad would regularly bring books home for me to read: history, geography, reading, spelling, and more. He watched me line my dolls up side by side in front of a black board and teach them Arithmetic and Spelling. "Poopie, one day you will be a teacher." I was not too happy about that because the kids in school did not treat the teachers well. Besides, I did not like to talk much and teachers talked all the time. In Catholic Elementary School, quietness got me picked on and teased regularly; I was called the "goody-two-shoes" of the school. So I hated school. I did not fit in and children took many opportunities to degrade me. This is my first opportunity to be aligned with Jesus.

While in junior high school I thought about being a nun because the nuns always helped people. When asked what I wanted to be when I grew up I told

Miss Sullivan, my 6th grade teacher that I just wanted to help people. I did not know how I would help people but I just knew I had to help people. I always stood up for the underdog, no matter who it was. I spent some weekends at the Little Sisters of the Poor, a home for the aged run by nuns beginning on Friday after school and leaving Sunday morning in time for Mass my mother made sure of that. My tasks included, doing hair in the salon, feeding and cleaning up behind those who had trouble eating on their own, and the hardest thing I had ever done was to wipe an old lady's behind after a bowel movement. She was grumpy and yelling at me to wipe lower, go lower! My classmates who were volunteering with me refused to do the job and stood outside in the hall laughing and making sound affects. I did not know that there was a nun watching me outside the door as well. She sent the other girls on their way. When I finished the old lady was still fussing, "You can't leave the pot stinkin' like that!" Sister walked in and said that she would take it from here. She said, "Wanda, I am proud of you, you stood up and did your duty." I knew I would make a great nun, this had to be the ultimate test. I walked around the house practicing being holy by putting a long scarf around my head and letting it hang down my back like a nun's veil then I folded my hands in front of me and walked around with a pious look on my face. My mother was tickled about the idea of her daughter being a nun but of course, dad was not thrilled. Dad sorta' won out thanks to high school where I found boys, boys, and more boys. I was definitely not going to become a nun.

It seems that the Holy Spirit spoke to me throughout my youth I just didn't know it, "Oh that today you would hear his voice, 'Harden not your hearts as at the rebellion in the day of testing in the desert . . ."—Hebrews 3:8 My desert testing had begun.

The Making of A Revolutionary

The grounding that your parents or guardians give you from the time that you come to the age of reasoning is very important to how you will live as an adult. I was raised to respond, "yes maam, and yes sir, please and thank you." I could not interject myself in grown folks conversations but I sure learned a lot by being the "child-fly-on-the wall". I heard my parents and their friend's talk about the movement that was going to change things for colored people. They sipped their liquor and played the phonograph while seeming to rejoice about a man named Martin Luther King, Jr. I remember wanting to be at that pool where he spoke about dreaming, but Dad said we could see better looking at it on television. I loved hearing the grown folks' intellectual discussions and I also loved how they partied.

I was raised on music. Music is my love. There was always music in my house. I learned early how to work the phonograph. I loved to sing. I belonged to the Holy Redeemer school choir from 6th grade to 12th grade, joined the St. Patrick's Academy high school choir, and then later in my adult life the St. Thomas More Catholic Church choir. Oh yes! Music made my heart leap for joy and I loved to sing! (Oh my, hello St. Cecilia!) I did not say that I "could" sing but I loved singing anyway. At home when I was not listening to Elvis Presley, Brook Benton, Ray Charles, and Ella Fitzgerald I made up my own songs and would dance to them. The nuns at my elementary school played classical music everyday at lunchtime, Beethoven, Mozart, and others, not to mention show tunes. I remember seeing some guys who went to school with me who said that they were the only guys in their neighborhood who knew and loved Beethoven and Mozart. Yes and I also love to dance. There is nothing more freeing than dancing. In high school I went to (as I date myself) "Sock Hops" which were informal high school dances.

I would not deal with a boy who could not dance . . . I figured for a man to be without rhythm was sacrilegious.

Yes I was the typical teenager: partying, dancing, laughing, "jone'in" . . . "you smell like, or you so ugly . . . ." I remember going on a blind date/double date when I was a junior in high school. My girlfriend knew her date but I had no clue about mine. We drove around the city visiting folks and looking for a party. Oh, my outfit was "hooked up" for that time period. My purple "granny" midi-skirt had the split up the front and my black long sleeve "popcorn" blouse was unbuttoned just a little to show the Catholic girl's forbidden cleavage. I felt I was too dressed to just ride around town. We ended up at this house where obvious necking was suppose to take place. Well, God was working on me then because I was not allowing somebody I did not know to lay hand one on me. This was the night of my first intense begging for God's help. An older man came in the front door with two one-gallon zip lock bags and he placed them on the coffee table and said, "Would you like some?" One bag held reefer and the other cocaine. My girlfriend panicked and began to loudly inquire as to what was in the bags as she began to hyperventilate. I remember hearing in my mind, "God please just get me out of here and back home with my mama and daddy please." I told the drug dealer, "No, I had some earlier, but thanks!" My girlfriend looked at me with shock and I told her that if she did not shut up I was going to knock her out. The next week at school I threatened to break her neck if she ever exposed me to danger like that again, knowing I would never go out with her again anyway. God was in the midst of a nasty situation that could have gone south very quickly. Amazing how your first encounter with God is when you need to be rescued quick, fast, and in a hurry, but then that is how the door of acknowledgement is opened.

I had some great friends and not so great friends at St. Patrick's Academy. I entered the school with reservation. I was sent to St. Pat's, a business high school, because nuns told my parents that I had a low I.Q., so I would not be able to hold my own in college and it would be more productive to direct me to a secretarial career. In elementary and junior high I was a "D"—"F" student. I was considered a slow learner. I was also overweight. I was 162 ½ pounds in the sixth grade. In the summer between leaving junior high and going to high school I lost weight. Thanks to the nuns, who directed my mother to take me to Children's Hospital, thanks to the doctor, who fed me placebo's, and thanks to my mother, who prepared the dietary meals that I hated I started high school weighing 115 pounds. You would think I would have been elated and running out to shop for a new wardrobe but instead I felt abnormal because I saw my bones and felt as if I was missing something . . . cushion, something. Doctors and society seem to think that once anyone loses poundage that they will automatically enjoy the thinner body, enjoy being like the models on the "catwalk", enjoy being like everyone else. Well, not in my case. I would have appreciated counsel on my sudden metamorphosis, I never wanted to be like everyone else, and I still weighed more than the other girls in my 9th grade class. Once I became comfortable in my skin I realized that I looked good in my hip-hugger, bellbottom jeans and my white midriff that showed my stomach. This style sounds familiar doesn't it? My self-esteem slowly rose.

High school was exciting and an awakening to new things for me. Lordy! The Civil Rights Movement was moving, the Black Panther Party was marching, and black people were in vogue. I donned the Angela Davis (Panther Party freedom fighter) Afro hairstyle with big hoop earrings. I would sit on the corner of 9th and F Streets, N.W., in downtown Washington, D.C., and watch the Panthers sell their newspapers. I was also proud of the fact that in D.C. the Panthers started a breakfast program for poor young children who left home most mornings hungry. Later they included an after-school tutoring program. **I JUST HAD TO BE A REVOLUTIONARY TOO!** The quiet, shy little grade school girl was going out and the revolutionary was coming in. In my sophomore year of high school six black students (out of a class of 21 students) held an in class protest because we were not allowed to go to the Martin Luther King Day Celebration. The nuns did not know what to do with us and we liked it that way. The homeroom Sister went to get the Principal and the Principal came in shrieking, "WHAT IS GOING ON IN HERE?!" I spoke up, "Why do we have to always hear about George crossing the Delaware, when are we going to learn about what our people (black people) did in history?" I took it further than Martin Luther King, Jr. I took her to what I yearned for in the deepest recesses of my soul. I took my first great revolutionary stance! I had arrived on the forefront of the revolutionary movement that definitely was not going to be televised it was going on live and in living color in my classroom. Of course we did not get a response from the nun but my parents got a phone call. *"We thought Wanda was a good girl."* My father answered the Principal, *"Wanda **is** a good girl and when **are** you going to teach her about her people?"*

Sometimes, you have to reach back in your history to know who you are before you can receive your Call in Africa it is called "Sankofa." You have to appreciate your journey, your past, before you can move forward into your future. You have to say, "Ahhh, that was an interesting mountain moment". If you do not recognize your lessons then you will definitely repeat them at a more intense level than before. It is the lessons that you learn from the mountain that make you strong. *"But Saul increased all the more in **strength**, and confounded the Jews who lived in Damascus by proving that Jesus was the Christ." (Acts 9:22 NRS)* I wanted to confound someone as a new revolutionary. How can you stand in your Call if you are not standing strong? How can you stand on the front line of the battlefield with Jesus if you do not have the strength of a Moses, David, or a Vashti, who refused to be humiliated by her drunken husband. We have heard this quote forever, *"If you don't stand for something you will fall for anything."*

I had no plans of falling for anything. If I was going to fall I had to fall on my terms. Revolutionaries throughout history always had courage and stood with their backs straight against the adversary and usually revolutionaries stand-alone. Audre Lorde said, *"When I dare to be powerful, to use my strength in the service of my vision, then it becomes less and less important whether I am afraid."* My youth and my vision guarded me from fear. I had a vision! I had to stand up to the St. Patrick's establishment and stand up for my people. I saw myself in war gear ready to take whatever they dished out. This was my first time standing under Ephesians 6 . . . I put on the whole armor!

There were moments in my young life when the earth's surface just seemed to appear out of nowhere but serious Christians know that faith can move mountains that suddenly appear. This was a time in my life when I had not grasped an awareness of the power of God for myself. I was still riding on my mother's beliefs. How many of you know that you have to have a personal relationship with God in order to master the mountain?

After graduating from St. Pat's on a Sunday, I was working at the Federal Bureau of Investigation (FBI) on Monday. It was amazing that I took the job at all but I wanted a good job and I wanted my **OWN** money, besides there was a television show on at that time called the "F.B.I.", which glamorized the job even more for me and besides my brother and his buddies worked there so I was going to work there too. Federal government recruiters came to our school and I made my choice my first interview was with the F.B.I., I was so excited because I knew it was a cinch to get a clerk-typist position. I loved to type and I continually challenged myself to go faster and faster. I went to that job interview dressed like a young professional ready to answer all the questions posed to me. All I could think of was the money, new friends, the money, and **the money**. Well, before getting the job I had to embrace another mountain. I went to F.B.I. Headquarters on Pennsylvania Avenue and all I could do upon entering the building was look up at the high hallway ceilings, look down at the marble floors and the big desks and I was captivated. I approached the secretary's desk and told her who I was and she told me to go right in. I walked in with my back straight and my mind focused on getting the job. The office was also palatial. It was your typical museum sized room trimmed in beautiful woodwork and marble floors. I suddenly lost my confidence. The mountain was rising up out of the marble. In the middle of the room was this oak executive desk that seemed tiny compared to the expansiveness of the room. In front of the desk about one step away was the chair that I was asked to sit on. I sat with my back straight, crossed my legs at the ankles (like the nuns taught me), and folded my hands in my lap. Mr. Smith (not his real name) asked me some basic interview questions and I gave the answers that would guarantee me the job. Then Mr. Smith stood up, walked around to the front of the desk and sat on it directly in front of me. Right after he told me to relax his hands found their way to my body; first he rubbed my face, then my neck, and walking behind my chair then, his hands were on my shoulders and traveled down my back. My mind and body became one—one with the chair, one with the wood, one with the marble. I could not decide if I wanted to leap off that cliff but it was just TOO slippery or maybe I could leap over one of those tall trees but they were just TOO tall. I could do nothing. Suddenly, Smith turned away and said, *"Ok, you can go. We will be in touch with you."* Shoot! I thought I had already been in touch! I got up and walked out of the room closing the door behind me. I remember looking with disbelief at the secretary who returned my stare with a look that said, *"I am so sorry."* I felt sorry for her that she had to put up with Smith on a daily basis. I still wanted the job and I knew that I would not be working on Pennsylvania Avenue with Mr. Smith.

Was I on guard during my tenure with the Bureau? Nope. There is that youth thing again. Did I forget the experience? Nope. Do you know what it is like to store mountains in the mind? People do it everyday and wonder why they develop illnesses like cancer, psychoses, and neurosis, hives, and more. I just moved forward having no idea that this was another strengthening moment in my life. Never did I wonder about where God was or even talk to God about this outrageous experience. Many people live day to day and never acknowledge God who lives inside of them. I use to wonder how I got through so much without acknowledging God and still overcame the mountain experiences. I know, now, that God was walking with me the entire time. He coated me so that foolishness did not pierce my heart and my mind. When the old folks say that God looks out for babies and fools, never was there ever a truer statement.

I stayed with the Bureau for eight or nine months before I left. The entire time I was in high school my mother gave me lecture after lecture about being a good girl and not to let boys put their hands on me and also *"DON'T GET PREGNANT!"* I did pretty well at following orders. I did not get pregnant in high school I waited until I started working. Seven months into the job I spent morning after morning nauscious. My father told my mother to take me to the doctor's office. In the doctor's office is where I heard the words, *"Well, your daughter is pregnant."* I thought my mother was going to leap off the chair and beat Satan right out of me. Oh and I saw this mountain grow even higher than any I had ever seen before. In 1973 at the F.B.I. you could not be unwedded and pregnant you would be fired and if you left within the first year of your employment you could not come back because of the cost of the extensive background check. It was also because of a moral superiority that seems almost hilarious when you think about who was in charge of the Bureau at that time. J. Edgar Hoover was no saint people!

I had a few months to go to reach that one-year mark but morning sickness would not let it happen. I quit the Bureau. I had my daughter Wanisha Marie Brown April 30, 1974. She died from S.I.D.S (Sudden Infant Death Syndrome) three months later. I sure could have used some faith right about then, instead I cried and I cried some more. It is unimaginable to know trials and tribulations, situations that cause suffering and not know Jesus. The snow on my mountain was melting and I was sliding down on the jagged edges of the mountain. I had to put behind me the social plague of man called "judgment." I went through the pregnancy unable to go to church because my mother said that it would be brazen for me to go up into church with my belly poking out and not married. I then thought that my other friends and family were ashamed of me, after all the job thought I was a disgrace and my mother seemed to be ashamed. I do not believe it is all right for young girls to get pregnant at whim like they do today. Young girls get pregnant to hold on to the popular boy that they had for one night of ecstasy. They get pregnant to increase their welfare check. They get pregnant because they want someone to love and they have no idea that they can love themselves so completely because the God who is complete and Divine dwells inside of them. We have to teach our girls this self-love and not shame. Our parents, my parents, gave me everything that they knew how to give me. I thank God that my mother taught me the work ethic and to never give up. My dad taught me that knowledge is power and reading is fundamental. My father did not appreciate the nuns telling us that I did not have the intelligence to go to college because he knew his baby was brilliant! I had not yet learned about the love inside of me and the gift of God's brilliance that lay dormant within me.

After Wanisha died it was a year before I returned to the workforce. I had to spend time hurdling this mountain by spending quiet time wondering how I got to where I was and where I was going from here.

A Writer's Soul

After the pain of loss poetry arose from my heart. Poetry is like music—the rhythm and rhymes—the messages of hope, love, strength, and pain. I read poetry in school, e.e. cummings, Browning, Shakespeare, Dickerson, and James Weldon Johnson. One day my God's genius opened up inside of me and I was composing. My classmates loved my work, but one of my classmates snidely said, *"Well, that's fine, but if you don't know Nikki Giovanni then you don't know poetry."* I wondered who was this Nikki Giovanni. I found out that she was spending time with the Panther Party and when I read her work I was mesmerized. I thought, *"This sister is powerful! Her writing could be called 'raw truth'!"* Nikki wrote about what directly affected blacks and what blacks were afraid of saying openly, she did it through the art form called poetry. I knew I had to be a revolutionary poet.

"Strike a blow
take a stand
bleed the blood
fight the fight
fear no man
beat a drum
make a plea
saddle up
move 'em out
stand for something
fall for nothing
in the name of justice

because you can
for the future
for the cause
strike a blow
strike a blow
strike while the iron is hot
strike
for the sake of . . .
stand and bleed . . .
we need a revolution ya'll!

I wrote and wrote and wrote in wild abandon never thinking about publishing any of it. My poetry was for my friends and for self-gratification. Later in my journey I learned what to do with the words that I put to paper. In the beginning was the word and my life and the life of others was about to begin again through my words granted to me by my Spirit Father.

Poetry is a dance of truth—a rhythm of emotions—the voice of the people. The flow of words exposes the breath and depth of the composer's emotions and passion. The poet is the town crier or the Griot. Conscious poetry comes from God, the words can create new life, the words can expose lawlessness, and they rally a nation. In the first Chapter of the Gospel of John it says, *"In the beginning was the Word, and the Word was with God, and the Word was God . . . All things came to be through him, and without him nothing came to be. What came to be through him was life and this life was the light of the human race . . . ."*

I lived and breathed poetry. It did not have to rhyme, but it had to have reason. I had to give my words to a larger audience so I joined a troupe of revolutionary poets. We were called the "Quest Poetry Series." We traveled throughout the Washington, D.C. metropolitan area reciting radical truths. I believe this was my second opportunity to preach truth, I see that now the first was the stand I took in the classroom for Martin Luther King Day. I was able to stand and speak out before crowds because of my affiliation with Toastmasters International an organization that teaches you to speak to one as well as one thousand. From the base of the Monument to churches throughout the Washington metropolitan area and even the palatial halls of government my poetry was heard. Eventually, I learned how to put my poetry in print so I could self-publish it. Only individual pieces were professionally published. Quest members eventually went their separate ways. I continued reading my word at local clubs and for those who cared to listen.

In 1987 I joined another law enforcement agency where employees came to know me as a poet. I was called upon to recite my work for various celebrations such as Black History Month, Women's History Month, and any other celebration that called for a poet to be taken from the shelf and dusted off. I say that because it seemed that the only time that people *really* wanted to hear poetry was for celebrations of the self.

The D.C. resemblance of the Harlem Renaissance period was no more. The D.C. Black Repertoire Company that opened us up to the African American arts was gone. It seemed to be replaced by the world of technology—everything has to be done with a quickness yet, how do you rush a masterpiece, how do you rush the arts? Gone was the power of the Negro arts, plays, poetry, and the cabarets that gave new life to downtrodden spirits with the greats, Duke Ellington, Ella Fitzgerald, and Count Basie then there were the books and platforms that gave us the genius of Claude McKay, Fannie Lou Hammer, Gwendolyn Brooks, and Langston Hughes. There is a genius in the new technology but it does not grasp the nature of a person like the passion during the Harlem Renaissance period. Well, my spirit felt driven to express itself more, to continue the D.C. Renaissance passion. I felt a need to write more but I had to do more than write poetry, I had to teach people how to maintain their passion for living a fulfilled life.

In my position in the government I became a trainer in soft skills. I developed and wrote lesson plans, outlines that trainers use to teach a course. I enjoyed developing courses that when delivered had the possibility of changing a person's behavior or thought processes. Can you hear the minister coming out? I got a rush seeing the light come on in someone's eyes when they acquired a new way of doing things. It was a light that told me that the person understood a process and was willing to carry that process out back on the job maybe in their everyday lives.

I am talking about variations of my gift as a writer because it is important for us to know the gifts God gives us. It is a gift that I use in my ministry. The New Testament Book of James says, *". . . all good giving and every perfect gift is from above . . . ." (1:17)* God gave me a perfect gift in writing and teaching. Remember, my dad said, *"Poopee, one day you will be a teacher."* All of us have at least one perfect gift sometimes more. That one perfect gift is what you use to make a living and to Evangelize (bring souls to Christ), it is what you use to bring people closer to their God-purpose, if you, yourself understand the God inside of you. When you give what has been given to you just to please God you will be rich in blessings. I always knew as a little girl that I had to help people but I did not know how I would help them; I just knew I had to. Everywhere I went to read poetry, reading words that came from my heart, that came from social issues, which saddened me or made me angry because people were hurt, abused, oppressed, or downtrodden the revolutionary in me raised a word of justice, a rhyme of freedom, and a rhythm of awakenings, I knew I helped somebody.

On my government job because my specialty is soft-skills, i.e., telephone techniques, professional image, diversity, communication skills, or self-esteem I could help awaken people even further. Can you see that being a trainer took me closer to the skill of preaching. I wrote and spoke words that gave people new knowledge, relief, and satisfaction to their souls.

I liken life to being in "JC" *(Jesus Christ)* University. My life curriculum of Jesus lessons were lessons that prepared me to resurrect into God's purpose for me. This journey is long and quite bothersome at times. Here I was reaching a broad economical, cultural, and social group through poetry and teaching, you would think that I would be satisfied! Dear God! There has to be more! Instead of reaching higher and farther for God I reached for man.

Lost In Man

"One evening David got up from his bed and walked around on the roof of the palace. From the roof he saw a woman bathing . . . The woman was very beautiful and David sent someone to find out about her."
—(2 Samuel 11: 2-3 NAB)

David was lusting after Bathsheba, the wife of Uriah, who was an officer in David's army. David sent Uriah to the front lines of battle where he was sure to be killed. David had impregnated Bathsheba and he loved her and he just had to possess her so killing off her husband to get him out of the way seemed logical in his possessed mind. David didn't love her that much because he tried to send Uriah home to be with his woman so he would think that he got her pregnant but that didn't work so murder was the next alternative and it was premeditated at that!

So often we think that we need to possess someone. Think about the word "possess." Merriam-Webster On Line defines "posses" as to have and hold as property; control firmly, or dominate, to bring or cause to fall under the influence. Sounds like a form of slavery doesn't it? It is slavery. Whenever someone seeks to control your entire life dismissing your dreams, wants, desires, and that which was given to you by God, as order and decency is slavery, possession, and evil. This cannot be called trust or love. David had a spirit of lust; he thought that it was love, so he possessed Bathsheba, who gave herself over to the possession. They both acted in opposition to their godliness—their higher consciousness. If David acted out of a godly conscious, out of Godly love, he would have respected the relationship that Bathsheba had with her husband. He could have fallen in love with her but God-love would not allow him to act on that love but respect the sacredness of that marriage. Now that's love!

In my mid 20's through my mid 40's I did not focus on love that came from God rather I sought to possess the love of man at all cost because I needed to serve myself—my desires. Even worse I thought that I loved myself by treating myself to whichever man I wanted no matter what his commitment elsewhere. I was possessed. The whole idea behind telling you my story is to show you that God does not always Call the saved and sanctified folk. God wants to be glorified. God wants his children to know that it is never too late to make a positive change even if you do not know that you need to change. Let me tell you, I had no clue that I needed to release the spirit of lust. At this time I was juggling three relationships at once and enjoyed being served. It would not seem that I would make minister material . . . but God. ***BUT GOD!*** Remember the Bible said that David was a man after God's own heart even with all of David's faults.

I loved, love. I loved what I thought love meant flowers, gifts, kisses, hand holding, and sex. The idea of walks by the water under the moonlight just thrilled me! I had a Hollywood concept of love. I had a fairy tale idea of relationship.

I got married on my fairy tale notion. I married someone who was a best buddy and unfortunately he and I realized too late that all we were meant to be was buddies. We went through one day of pre-marriage pastoral care, which had no impact on the reality of our lives. As a matter of fact the only thing that we remember was a couple that sat in the circle with us kissing and petting as if they were home in bed. The priest standing across the room did not notice until another couple brought it to his attention.

We got married anyway because we were comfortable with each other but really did not know our individual selves. We believed in God based on our parent's knowledge of God, which they instilled in us. The marriage was actually over in the first year but we stayed together for five more years. I became pregnant in the first year of our marriage and we were happy about having a son. You need to know that children do not sustain a marriage, God does. My ex-husband and I are still supportive of each other and we still guide our son as a team. What did we learn? That you must know God's desire for your life and you must know who you are in the power of God before you join with another. Even though a marriage does not work out the children should not suffer. If you bring children into a relationship know that God has given you a gift and the responsibility to rear them in God's will and in God's way. Did I seek counsel? Yes I did prior to separation. I went to see a Brother who was assigned to the Roman Catholic Church that I was attending and after telling him the situation he was confounded but he told me I could get an Annulment. It is actually called a "decree of Nullity" which means that on the day that vows were taken there was an element missing in one or both parties that would hinder a life long marriage. The reasoning would have to be proven and then taken through a Tribunal process. This was an arduous process that I was not willing to go through.

After separating from my husband I continued on in other fairy tale relationships with three men. Ricky, Adam, and Ajiri. Why did I need three men? When one was not available then another one would be. You have to know that I was possessed by a variety of spirits: lust, low self-esteem, depression, and alcoholism, but sex was at the forefront of each fairy tale. I used sex as a drug to make me feel good. The reality is sex did not help as a matter of fact my feelings did not change for the better but in actuality got worse.

Adam I knew for years, our relationship was an on again, off again, relationship. We partied together but I never knew where he lived nor could I ever call him. Women know the signs of a married man or a man living with someone and this was a sign that I chose to ignore.

Then there was Ricky whom I met soon after separating from my husband. I met him in my depression and alcoholism. Ricky was my life coach and "sugar daddy." I was never broke. Ricky introduced me to my African heritage and the idea that I was a queen worthy of love and respect. **Queen?** I thought this man was crazy! He gave me books to read and he guided me to what it meant to take care of myself physically, mentally, and spiritually. He was my nurturer for a season and he also was a male presence for my 3-year-old son. Oh yeah, Ricky left his wife, went back to his wife (for the kids), left, went back over and over again, and it was surely getting old.

Finally, there was my African prince (not really), Ajiri from West Africa who was single (AT LAST!) He was peaceful and quiet and I was drawn to his quiet nature. But Ajiri was a selfish single man. I guess this explained him being single.

All three of these men brought something to the table. No, really they did! They all showed me varying levels of spirituality but they used their individual knowledge of spirituality to control and/or to possess me. This revelation did not come to me until years after letting them go. Psalm 22: 13-15 says, *"Many-bulls surround me; fierce bulls of Bashan encircle me. They open their mouths against me, lions that rend and roar. Like water my life drains away; all my bones grow soft. My heart has become like wax it melts away within me."* Adam spoke compassionately to me when I was troubled just like Jesus but unlike Jesus when I appeared to be getting strong he used the knowledge of my weaknesses against me. He relished controlling/possessing my thoughts and actions. Then Ricky saw me as a student—a project—a creation that he formed and fashioned. He wanted to be my god but with the capital "G." He opened my eyes to who I was spiritually. God used him to show me that I was a good woman and that I should want for nothing. Unfortunately, when his life began going into the toilet he wanted to take me to the toilet with him. The spirit that possesses man to rape a woman is unimaginable but that is what Ricky did to me. He no longer had control over his family or his life so he had to exert control over something, someone, with the ultimate act of control, rape. I trusted this man with my life. I was devastated but not enough to go to the throne of Grace! A man who taught me that I deserved to be treated like a queen showed me that I was really still a slave.

Lastly, Ajiri was a man who taught me meditation at its highest. This man showed me how to communicate with another person mentally without uttering one word. I remember him telling me, *"Tomorrow at some point in the day call my name a few times in your mind and I will hear you in my mind."* Deep isn't it? Yes, but it is possible. I learned that most of us possess the ability to communicate telepathically. How many times have people told you that they were just thinking about you before you called? This is not a coincidence or happenstance. We are all connected. Ajiri, unfortunately, called me when he wanted something, sex, help him with a business venture, or to whine about his woes. I remember my mother saying, *"Wanda that man whines all the time."* How many know that I had to disconnect our mind-link?

One New Years Eve I decided enough was enough and thanks to God and Ricky I realized that a queen deserved better than this. I dumped all three of my suitors—my lions that rend and roared. I let go of the fairy tales. I was free for the first time in a long time. I know I had a testimony for sisters and I knew I would one day help to guide women toward who they really are. Each of these men represented rocky peaks and put together they were mountainous terrain surrounded by an exploding blizzard knocking me from peak to cliff, from cliff to peak. I was bruised, banged-up, and tired. These men were seasonal, some timey, and they brought knowledge about what they were made of also what I was made of. It is said that the energy that you put out, your thoughts, your actions, and your words, is the same energy that you get back. It was time for me to look at who Wanda Cecelia (Brown) Outlaw really was. I needed to be on my own out in the world receiving what God had just for me.

Breakthrough

So far, I have painted a picture for you of some mountainous moments in my life. I showed the mountains as hurdles to climb over, to get around, or to go through. I slipped, I fell, and I got back up and kept facing them. I have no regrets about my life and there is still much that I didn't share. It is at this point in the story where I need to show you that God wanted me to see mountains differently. God wanted me to see that the mountains and I could be one if I looked through spiritual eyes, godly eyes and not with eyes fashioned by the world. I had to learn that I was in the world and not of the world.

In a spiritual discipline a mountain represents a higher state of mind. When your mind is at a higher place you have thoughts of God's Divinity, you have thoughts of God's Truths, and your mind is awakened to a purpose that God has just for you. When the mountain is seen as a sacred state of being you become less attached to mortal thoughts and desires and you begin to embrace spiritual thoughts and desires.

It was on the mountain where Jesus sat down and cured the people and fed the thousands. Jesus took Peter, James, and John to the mountain and transfigured before their eyes—Jesus changed his appearance supernaturally. Jesus experienced fully the flow of God's power through his body. We can experience the same transformation by elevating our thoughts. My consciousness was expanding to capture mountains differently. When life and my weaknesses sought to take me down it was in the mountains where I was being rescued. I always saw mountains as obstacles to get over, to knock down, or run around never did I see the mountains as a place of peace where God was waiting for me to come and be transformed.

January 2, 1989, my father, Augustus King Brown died. He lived two years in a paralyzed state induced by a series of strokes. I moved back home to live with my mother when my father went to a VA Medical Center in his final years. In the latter part of July 1989 I received a call from a former school friend who later became one of my spiritual guides. Karen Kramer called me, "GIRLLLL! Have I got a church for you! It's revolutionary just like you! You gotta' go—please say you will go!" Karen told me that the name of the church was "Imani Temple." She said that a former Roman Catholic Priest named George Stallings started the church. I had never heard of him before or so I thought. I did not remember that I saw him previously at my cousin's church, St. Theresa's of Avila in S.E. Washington. I also heard about him from a nun friend of mine who said that he was a brilliant man, a strong preacher, and an Evangelizer. She said that he might be putting something together. I did not piece together that this was the same man until after I had been a member of Imani for a while.

Karen, her husband, and children took me to Imani Temple. I had never seen anything like it the parking lot was full and packed buses were pulling up to the doors. It was as if the people were running for their lives, with anticipation in their veins, but anticipating what? The place was packed from top to bottom, but there were also television cameras along the wall. In this century no Roman Catholic Priest of this magnitude had broken away and started his own sect. It was not easy, the death threats came oh so regularly to him. All of a sudden I heard drums and I thought it was thunder rolling down from above, unified voices began chanting, "Ago . . . Ago Ahmee!" from the African Twe language. The drums were getting louder and louder, behind the drummers was a long procession of people swaying back and forth like trees in a cool breeze, they were chanting, smiling, rejoicing, and banners were held high, not your regular churchy banners but red, black, and green banners. Oh my God, the colors of Liberation! The choir was moving in rhythm, to and fro, incense barrers, and someone carrying the Gospels Book (the Word of God) high. **IT WAS MAGNIFICENT!** I felt as if I had come home, I was free! My soul was stirred and I understood what I saw on hundreds of faces, it was the anticipation of possibly seeing the face of God while cradled in the arms of Mother Africa.

I frequently tell people what I consider to be my birth order:

1st a child of God
2nd an African
3rd a Woman

and then everything else. Titles have never meant much to me but I had to recognize God first and then the fact that I am an African. Some African Americans are quick to tell me that I was not born in Africa so I am not African. Once again, the foolishness of man and woman, the edicts of the world always want to dictate who we are and what we are. This revolutionary will not be put into a box of "should's or "ought's". My great grandmother and grandfather came to this country on slave ships. Phoebe and Walsh Thomas came from either Ghana or Sierra Leone *(Thank you Cousin Vanessa for the fact-finding.)* It is important that we define ourselves for ourselves and not allow man, woman, or institutions to define us.

I joined Imani Temple as a baby revolutionary and through great scripture teachings I excelled to a junior revolutionary. Imani Temple took stances against racism. I remember a Synod (general church meeting) held in Louisiana where all the Imani Temples across the nation convened to make new church laws and to fellowship. The clergy got word that a young man was shot in the back after running from the police. They shot him in a field as he was trying to get home to his mother. They say that they arrested him but could not tell his family for what. The question of the day was, *"How did he escape?"* It was rumored that the African-American boy was dating the white Sheriff's daughter. The clergy got the Call to March and MARCHED we did . . . clergy and congregations car pooled to the church that called the march and we lined up. We walked, we walked, and we walked. This was my first march. Unfortunately, my shoes were not made for marching but there were men who slowed up their pick-up trucks and pulled others and myself aboard. I loved this! We also had the experience of white men and women yelling slanders, riding their trucks up next to ours close enough to allow their growling dogs to snipe at us. We did not fear . . . I did not fear. I understood at last what my family/ancestors went through. I was grateful for this moment but saddened that it had to happen in the 90's.

I am so grateful for Imani Temple and all the relationships and ministries that God led me to. God guided me along with two sisters who sandwiched me in one Sunday morning and they asked me, *"Don't you want to join the Lector Ministry?"* In the Lector Ministry laymen and laywomen proclaim (read) the unadulterated word of God during Mass. I remember thinking that I was not worthy to carry the Book of the Gospels in the procession, but I did it *(Thanks Sherrill and Kathy*).

They also taught me how to converse with God in prayer out loud. I was raised in the Roman Catholic Church where prayer was already mapped out, structured, and everyone recited the same words together. It was purposeful but I found another way to increase my relationship with God, it was more personal, and it was in the spirit of the African call and response. Imani Temple gave that to me. The Lector Ministry taught me to talk to God from my heart for myself, and others. The more I talked to God the more I wanted to talk to God. In the Roman Catholic Church the first and second readings were both taken from the Bible. In the African American Catholic Congregation's Imani Temple the first reading is from the Bible but the second readings are taken from African and African American writers throughout history as well as writers in the present times. When the Head of the Ministry learned about my poetry I was asked to write some of the second readings. What an honor! My gift that glorified God and liberated God's people went from the secular audience to the spiritual.

If you remember I said earlier that I was raised in a dual denomination household, mom was Roman Catholic and dad was Baptist. After getting older I always wanted the best of both my mother and my father. I enjoyed the loud rejoice, the praise and worship of the Baptist church and the bells, incense, and Cantoring of the Roman Catholic Church. I got all of that at Imani Temple. I still struggled to understand the "Shout" experience. I enjoyed watching the freedom of the people who experienced it; the ecstasy in their eyes and the screams of praise from their lips as well as a strange language that they spoke, not for the common ear but possibly for a spiritual realm to understand. I asked God timidly for the experience of the shout and if you but ask to the glory of God you will receive.

One Sunday I was scheduled to read the second reading. Whenever I proclaimed the word of God I included everything that I learned about delivering a speech from Toastmasters to how I recited my poetry. One Sunday I was reading a poem entitled, "Tambourines" and because the Lector Ministry believed in creativity in delivery two other Lectors played tambourines in the background while I read the poem. Something came over me in the proclamation of the poem. The congregation rose to their feet. While they were praising and the drums were beating I went back to my seat and sat down but something was going on. I had trouble sitting still. I shifted right—I shifted left. I looked at my sister Lector who sat beside me, she looked at me as if she knew what was about to happen. I started to rise off the chair and sat back down. I moved forward on the chair and then pushed back. I felt a stirring, a fire, throughout my body that I could not control. The next thing I remember was standing in a corner shaking and crying. I experienced my first shout! Alleluia! I was in the presence of God. I was touched by the Holy Spirit, oh my, my, my, the peace I felt afterwards is almost indescribable. I was not apart of the world any longer. I was awakened to a new mountain experience. I saw a mountain that served as a place of peace. I felt the salvation of the Lord. I felt freedom and I felt love and security all around me from the highest peak of a mountain! This came from God and not man. I had a breakthrough!

Did my lifestyle change? Not completely, not yet, but the portal had been opened and I no longer saw mountains as a barrier but a safe haven, a higher place from whence cometh my help. I was not yet where I ought to be but I thank God I was not where I use to be. I was on the road to salvation but I still had a ways to go.

God Uses The Government

"Let every person be subordinate to the higher authorities, for there is no authority except from God, and those that exist have been established by God."

—(Romans 13:1 NAB)

God even controls the government. There are many men and women in leadership, whether in government or corporate America, who think they have all power and authority but even they have to be subordinate to God. In spite of them God still maintains authority.

The beauty of working as a trainer, especially a soft-skills trainer is that you are always in demand. I traveled nationally and taught at support conferences using lesson plans that I wrote laced with motivational energy *(Yes daddy, I teach and travel).*

I was scheduled for three conferences traveling to places that I had never been, Palm Springs, California, Phoenix, Arizona, and Seattle, Washington. **IS GOD GOOD OR WHAT?! You bet God is!** I was scheduled for surgery between the second and the last trip. All three trips were three-day stints, fly in one day, teach the next day, and fly out the next day.

First trip: Palm Springs, California. Let me mention that flying made me crazy. The inside of a plane reminded me of a greyhound bus with wings. The first time that I had to fly for the government was to Detroit, Michigan and my family had to urge me on the plane on one end while the flight attendants coaxed me from the other end. When I finally got to my seat the flight attendant yelled, *"We got one!"* I was told to grip the seat and all would be well. Co-workers were trying to prepare me for my flight but when the bell went off to let us know to fasten our seat belts I leaped outside of my skin and sucked air. God put a nurturer beside me. He talked me through the entire trip to Detroit. I did improve as a passenger after a few more flights for the government and with the church.

The Palm Springs trip took me over water and yep, mountains. They were beautiful. I saw where the "purple mountains majesty" came from. Some of the mountains were really purple in color. I learned that it was sulfur that caused the color. Amazing! A cute little old lady sitting next to me pointed to the hills on our left at our beginning descent and told me that the house that looked carved out of the side of the mountain was Bob Hope's house. That was nice, but I was pre-occupied with how our jet was going to safely land in the middle of these hills. It was as if the plane had to become a helicopter and drop down instead of gliding in.

Lord knows, I was happy on the ground and breathing freely as sweat traveled down various crevices of my body. I stepped outside of the terminal to get a taxi and it was so very quiet. I had never heard or felt anything like it. There were no loud traffic noises, no sirens, and no one was speaking loudly. The taxi driver noticed my curious looks and answered my curiosity, *"Yeah, it is really quiet here—it's the first thing people notice when they leave the terminal."* It is an absolutely beautiful place, dry heat, sun, and palm trees.

Whenever I go into my hotel room before I unpack I bless the room from the door to the windows, north, south, east, and west. Then I set up an altar, which is my sacred place, my focus, for prayer and meditation. I opened the balcony curtains and there before me was an ugly, dusty looking wall. What kind of view is this?! All the beauty and serenity of Palm Springs and I get a dust wall. Something moved me closer to the balcony door. I opened it, stepped outside, and looked up. I was tickled. There, rising above me was a mountain. I was at the base of a mountain. I could almost reach out and touch it. I grabbed my camera and ran around to the back of the hotel and saw that it was a small mountain but nevertheless it was mine for three days.

It was here where I met a petite Asian woman named Miko. Miko was a Masseuse. I signed up for a full-bodied, Aromatherapy massage package that included a manicure and a pedicure. This was my first and last massage. I have got to do it again one day. She worked knots out of my body that I did not realize could be worked out. She said I had stress build up, which caused the knot in the back of my neck. I placed my hands and feet in soothing hot wax and then Miko put my hands in white wool mitts and my feet in booties—Oh Lord!. When she was done with me my feet had shrunk and my body was glowing . . . I was in Nirvana. If you want to show yourself love a massage, manicure, and pedicure is the way to go.

Second trip: Phoenix, Arizona. This has got to be the hottest place I have ever been. If hell is worse than this I know I am not going—Trust me! Imagine stepping from 70-degree temperature into 200-degree temperature. Oh wait! Stick your head into a freezer and then turn around and stick your head into an oven at 350 degrees. This was what I felt when leaving the terminal in Phoenix. People tell you how hot it can be but until you experience the desert heat you **really** don't know heat. Palm Springs was desert as well but not like Phoenix. I walked toward the automatic airport terminal doors with my bag in tow, a smile on my face, and pep in my step. The doors opened up, I glided through, and it felt like my face was melting. I screamed, dropped my bag, and grabbed my face. The taxi drivers were howling with laughter. Can you imagine? HOWLING while my face was melting. *"Taxi lady?!" "If you don't have air conditioning don't come near me!"* Go figure, I had to walk to the taxi stand because they were not permitted to pull up to the door. There is no running in 112-degree heat, so I sludged and dripped toward the taxi driver who did not bother to help me at least half the way by taking my bag.

The Phoenix desert was captivating. I began to wonder how Jesus did 40 days in the desert and then had to put up with the foolishness of Satan too! Anyway, there is something pure, a natural beauty, a purging about the desert.

I arrived at Pointe Hilton Squaw Peak Resort Hotel where they realize the severity of the heat so they give their customers a ride from one building to another on a golf cart. I was grateful to get inside my very cool suite. I did what I always do start at the front door and work my way through blessing and praying for the Holy Spirit to dwell in this place. I opened the curtain to the picture window beside the bed and off in the distance, only a parking lot and a block away was a mountain that they irreverently called "Squaw's Peak" which they have agreed to rename "Piestewa Peak" after a fallen solder, a Hopi Indian, Lori Piestewa, who was ambushed and killed with her fellow solders in Iraq. Yes, another mountain—a mountain of honor! Ok, God was sending me a message. First, I was at the base of a mountain and now the mountain was far off but I had a clear view. When I completed the teaching assignment I needed to go to my sacred place—my new mountain. Once I finish instructing a class I must go into solitude to replenish myself because I give up much of my spiritual energy to the teaching and to the participants. I sat in my room in the dark on the floor facing the mountain, with only a single candle for light. Suddenly a thunderstorm arose and the rain came, sheets of water, it was magnificent, majestic especially when the rain stopped and a cloud descended over the peak of the mountain exposing only the point of the peak. Then lightning came out of the cloud and danced upward and around the mountain peak. I was in awe. Instead of closing my eyes to commune with God in meditation I looked at the face of God in the lightning. I saw and felt God's energy and I saw God's smile light up the peak. I realized that God was giving me His razzle-dazzle, He was romancing my heart, my body, my mind, and my soul. Oh what a God we serve! Oh what a God I serve that He could love me so! I had never felt so fulfilled as I did in that moment.

All my life I have been open to new experiences, new ways of life, and different cultures. I believe that all cultures are connected through the Spirit of God. All religions that worship the God of goodness, holiness, and light, and the God who created all things seen and unseen are beneficial to the flow of the universe. Now, I know that sounds very "New Age" to some, but it is definitely Truth. Jesus said, *"I have other sheep that do not belong to this fold. These also I must lead, and they will hear my voice . . . ." (John 10:16 NAB)*

I believe that one group of sheep, the Native Americans or American Indians are among the most sacred people on the planet. The name by which they call God is "Great Spirit Father." The Native culture and the African culture are similar in their forms of worship and rituals; incense, dancing, drumming, belief that we walk as spiritual beings, honoring the elders, and celebrating the life of a deceased person rather than mourning the death. They also believe in "living" their religion and not "practicing" it.

I took an African name after prayer and meditation as well as to support my son who attended an independent African school. My name is Noni *(No-knee or Noh-nee)* from East Africa, specifically Tanzania, which means, gift of God. I love my name Noni, but it never felt complete until I went to Scottsdale, Arizona to look around and shop. I knew I was in Hopi Indian Territory. Hopi means, good, peaceful or wise. It always sickens me when people stereotype a culture especially when Christians label a culture "heathen" or "savage", but I guess we have all done it at some point and time. I also know that we must move pass it to glorify God in decency and in order. One way to prevent your self from doing this is to read about a culture or walk and talk with a culture. This is when appreciation begins. I mean "appreciate" not "tolerate." I don't know about you but I tolerate ants and bees at a cookout, I tolerate office assignments that I do not want to do. I do not want to be tolerated as an African-American I want to be appreciated.

In the specialty stores in Arizona the Native's art was sold and I often wondered how the money was divided between the merchant and the crafter because a lot of work went into crafting Kachina dolls, the jewelry, pots and more. Well, anyway, I was looking for a ring that emanated a spiritual energy. I stood at the counter and felt a presence at my back and I turned around and saw the most beautiful, most graceful looking "Kachina" doll on the shelf. Kachina translates as "spirit being." There are Kachinas for every purpose and the dolls are used to teach the children their history. No two Kachina dolls were exactly alike. I asked the store clerk who was she as I pointed to the Kachina covered with black crow feathers and her dress was black made in a hide material. It was stunning and I have never seen the same doll carved the same way again. I kept asking, who is she? He said that is Crow Mother, the Mother of all the Kachinas, and Mother of the Whipper Katsinam Family. Later I found out that she is well versed in moral principles and virtues of life and she was also considered a teacher and a healer. All I knew was that every time I turned away from Crow

Mother Kachina I was nudged, urged, to turn back around to face her. I felt as if I was receiving energy or maybe a blessing. The store clerk watched me do this dance of back and forth and said, *"She is calling you."* I thought, "Well, other spirits have called before so why not one more." I did not purchase the doll but I did research Crow Mother. I knew she and I were becoming spiritual mother and daughter so I took her name. Now, I am often called by my spiritual name that is oh so complete, "Noni Crowmother."

Well, I was given two mountains—two different views of a mountain, two perspectives of solitude, two visions of peace, and two microcosms of heaven. Metaphysically speaking two levels of God conscious-existence. I was being shown how to survive in ministry—how to serve in the world and not lose my mind. God gave the words to one of my spiritual guides. He said, *"Sister, you stay on the mountain until you have to leave the mountain to serve the people and then you return to the mountain with God."* I was being shown how to remain strong, focused, and sane in an insane world, but why me? What was all this about and what was my purpose in all of this? Well, I would have plenty of time to think about it. I would spend 3-weeks in my house healing from a hysterectomy.

Dear God what do you have for me? What am I to do?

Only A Spirit Can Embrace Spirits

Scriptures tell us that we must worship God in spirit and in truth. I learned that we are not human beings practicing to be spiritual rather spiritual beings practicing to be human. We are spirit first.

Knowledge of being a spirit was never a new thing to me. I always thought of myself as a spirit and was always acquainted and comfortable with the idea of spirits being present in another dimension that exists beside our human world. My family told me stories about people who were born with a veil over their faces. It was a light film that covered the baby's face that the doctor had to remove. It is said that those born with the veil could regularly see spirits. Sometimes certain gifts are inherited like being able to see or communicate with spirits. The Call to ordained ministry is believed by some to be inherited or a gift God chooses to give you. In my family there are cousins and aunts who could see spirits. There was an uncle who was a prophet and two cousins who are ministers, even my mother had her own spirit encounter. My mom told me stories about "Root" workers in the country and their powers but she said they could never be as powerful as God. Mom also told me about a visitation that she had from her deceased father who warned her about the difficulties that she would face in the future. She said granddad's steps were loud as he walked across the porch it shook and stopped outside her window but mom was not afraid she recognized his voice. If your spirit is familiar with the entity and you are grounded in God principles you have nothing to fear and your spirit will not fear. It is the same way when you have a personal relationship with God you become familiar with His voice even though you cannot physically see Him. Grandfather spirit was right mom faced many challenges in her life, but instead of fearing the future mom was reassured in the present that there were spirits who would be watching over her. Because of this and many discussions and encounters I did not fear spirits either.

My first experience with a spirit occurred after my first child, Wanisha Marie, died and I was depressed. I spent most of my time in my bedroom staring at the walls. One morning when I awoke I looked at the doorway and saw a large figure standing, smiling at me one minute, and then he would jump back as if playing peek-a-boo. It had the appearance of an angel, wings and all. The angel had a white aura so you could not tell what race it was but I knew it was a male. The angel did this every morning for about a week until I was laughing again and then my angel friend was gone, it was as if his sole mission was to save my heart and mind from self-destruction. I was grateful. I remember asking God to let me see my daughter grow up. *"How can you see someone dead grow up?"* I did not know how I just asked and God afforded me this gift ever since I was in high school. This was something I always asked of God when someone near me died. God obliged me in "Kairos" time—time not measured by a clock—also known as God's time. I saw my daughter go from a bassinet to womanhood in a matter of days. She finally spoke to me saying, *"Mama, I am going to be fine."*

I never feared spirits because they always nurtured me in some way. They were gentle with me because of my curiosity. I knew God was a Spirit and that God was a part of me. Then to later hear that we are spirit first it all tied together—it all made so much sense. Knowledge of a parallel world—a spirit world along side this natural world was wonderful in my mind. It means that you got folks who see what you cannot and they have your back. I later came to learn that all spirits were not good and holy but there were those spirits that were harmful and diabolical. I met these spirits as well.

By now you might be getting nervous about where my story is going and words like, "hocus-pocus" or "mumbo-jumbo" might be coming to your mind. It is very important to know or identify the gifts that God has given you as well as what God will give you if you but ask. Seeing spirits *(as they will or God wills)* is one of my gifts. I pray and discern about this gift constantly. Do I see them all the time? No, but I hear them often and I periodically see the holy ones in the form of gold and/or white lights that streak by every now and again. When verbal or physical harm is near I will see a dark mass move overhead. The first time I was attacked by a dark force I was shaken up but I never forget the power of God and the name of Jesus. In what seemed like a single hop from my bed to the other side of the room I began yelling, **"I BIND YOU UP AND CAST YOU OUT AND DOWN TO THE LOWEST PIT OF HELL IN THE NAME OF JESUS! THIS IS HOLY GROUND . . . GET OUT IN THE NAME OF JESUS!"** In the late night in my bedroom I have been pined to the bed and unable to speak because I was being choked. I always thought that a person broke into the house and had attacked me, I could not see them, but I could feel them . . . rough knobby extensions where there should have been arms and legs or multiple arms and legs, but I never forget to rebuke the evil force and call on the name of Jesus eventually seeing a dark form exit through a wall or the window. I believe in casting evil to the lowest pit of hell in Jesus' name! This was a lesson I learned early from my Imani Temple pastor and used quite often. I want you to know that evil spirits are REAL. When the evil one, Satan, knows that your journey is a high Calling to come he will step in to sway, discourage, **CRUSH** you so that you turn your back on your purpose . . . **DON'T YOU DO IT! ALWAYS FIGHT IN THE NAME OF JESUS** and victory will be yours and the glory will be Gods!

Wait! I want to give you one more spirit story because this one is the most powerful one for me to date. I was with a development team on Jekyll Island, Georgia and my supervisor and I finished early one day so we made haste to the beach. We had good novels to read and we were going to relax. I love the ocean water because it is good for locs and my locs hung down my back. I had a tee shirt with the picture of an African woman on it and I wrapped myself in African fabric as a "Lappa". It was a beautiful sunny and warm day. I got up off my towel, my supervisor was sitting on a large piece of drift wood reading, and I walked to the ocean waters to get wet. I bent forward and put my hair in the water, once, twice, when I came up the third time I heard chains. I looked out into the Atlantic and off to the right and there was a ship. Not any ordinary ship, it was a ship out of the 1700's or 1800's like a pirate ship or a slave ship that you would normally see in the history books or at a museum. I thought, how could this be—maybe it was one of those floating exhibits. I just kept staring at it and then I heard slapping sounds in the water. I looked left and there was an old, old, rowboat, bigger than what you see now and the slapping sound was its oars against the ocean. There were people in the rowboat, specifically, three white men and climbing out of the boat where slaves. How do I know they were slaves? I knew by what they were wearing, hardly anything. They were shackled around the neck, chained from wrist to feet. I focused on this one person, a woman, who stared at me and smiled. She was beautiful. She and I just stared at each other. I did not think to speak I was just taking in the vision that did not seem like a vision it seemed real seeing the men in shackles and the white men yelling and pushing them. I wondered why they did not touch her or yell at her. After she and I stared and stared, smiled and smiled she turned and followed the men up on the beach and into the woods and I watched them disappear. I turned to see the boat again but it too was gone. The beach and my supervisor came back into view. My supervisor, a God-fearing man, was staring at me and he knew I had seen something. *"Wanda, what did you see!?"* All I could say was, *"Huh?"* "What did you see? I know you saw something?" I told him about my vision, the woman and the ship, and the men on the big rowboat. We decided to return to the car and drive down the road to find some history. It seems that there use to be a plantation and a port down the road where a Frenchmen ran slaves. I was later told that people see the spirits of slaves on Jekyll Island all the time. It was said that they gave me a special gift. I was truly grateful.

Now, not to get too far off track in laying out my journey to accepting the "Call" you will see by-and-by why I had to familiarize you with this gift from God.

Transformation

I was working at another law enforcement Bureau, I was active at Imani Temple, and my mom was helping me to raise my son. All my adult life I was known as the one who smiles a lot even when times were rough. I traveled for the Bureau as a trainer but also as a motivational speaker. Some people had suggested that I become a minister and that I sounded like a minister. My response was always, *"Until Jesus sits down on my bed and tells me that I have to put on a collar, it ain't happening."* Shoot, I could help people without putting on a collar. I was teaching people how to be the best that they could be already, my poetry I used to enlighten people about the atrocities of the world and I was flowing in all of it. God and I were gellin'.

I had three main friends or confidants that I would talk to and hang out with. They nurtured me and I nurtured them. Then the climate changed, a seasonal shift was taking place and my life was about to turn upside down.

One friend always had a dream of opening a Christian bookstore that honored God. I heard her talk about the colors of the décor and how the store would look. One day I walked into her office to have one of our girly chats and she said, *"Sista, I'm outta' here. I am retiring."* She may never know how sad I was at hearing this news. Selfish, I know, but she was one of my mentors. I use to say when I grew up I wanted to be like her bold, decisive, intelligent, and beautiful. Little did I know I was already all of these things. Sista-friend left and then there were two. A brotha-friend was my official mentor on the job, but he became more. He became my spiritual guide who always told me that I could do anything and he never stopped encouraging me. One day he dropped a bombshell on me that he and his family were relocating to Seattle. My heart sank and the tears welled up inside of me. I thought, "Ok! Is this a conspiracy or what?!"

I do not take friendships lightly and I was never one to have a lot of friends I preferred having a few good friends because it is hard to nurture a friendship and I wanted to be good at it because God sent these people to me, to teach me, and to love me often times better than my own kin, so each time there was a divide I felt like a piece of me died. I have always been passionate about everything and everyone in my life. It is the best part of who I am.

So, you should know what is coming next. That's right, the last and final friend was about to exit my life. It was at this time that I was to have the hysterectomy, an overused form of healing women, but that's another story for another time. This friend and I were sister friends for quite a long time. I saw her as a big sister. I would have died for this sister and still would but now for different reasons. Her life became stressful for, I believe, various reasons and she began to ostracize me. This frightened me and I was not use to being so close to someone and then they pull back, pull away, and move apart from me. I did not know or understand what was going on. There was one tense moment after another between us then the big one came two days before my surgery. I was devastated and was not sure how we got to that place of discomfort, frustration, or miscommunication. None of it made sense, I did not feel fit for the fight, but all I knew was that all my friends were gone and I was on my own to face surgery.

WAIT A MINUTE! *YOU KNOW GOD, RIGHT?* The Holy Spirit had touched you, you got your shout on, and you were given the gift of Sight *(seeing spirits)* so where did all that go?! Well, I still had not matured spiritually, believe it or not. I was aware of gifts and abilities but its like the television shows where the cartoon character gets a new weapon and has not learned to use it effectively to thwart the enemy. Trust me, I was praying through it all but I was not sure I believed that God was listening or maybe God was doing a new thing in me and with me. I definitely did not understand. The Chinese have two words, a "Picogram", for the word "crisis", danger and opportunity. I was in crisis, I was in Kairos time—a moment in time that disrupted the normal flow. Psychologist might call it a "Paradigm Shift." I had to choose whether this disruption of my life was going to be danger or an opportunity. I sunk into an earth shaking mind altering and spirit stifling depression. I was in danger. I went to a place where many go and where more than a few do not make it out. I did not care if I lived or died.

I never had major surgery before this. My ignorance afforded me no fear of dying. I was oblivious to the idea of being cut open and parts of what supposedly made me a woman removed. When I look back I was crazy calm and somewhat jovial, I also had a cold and anyone who has had surgery knows that doctors do not perform surgery when other ailments are present, even if it is just a cold they lean toward canceling the procedure. Remember my state of mind, my friends were gone and I was not even sure about the confusion between my "bestest" friend and me. I was all right about dying. I had no idea why I infused so much drama—so much pain into my mind, heart, and spirit. If I had allowed the Spirit of God to speak to me . . . if I had gone to the holy mountain, my place of refuge instead of relying on my intelligence . . . Proverbs 3: 5-6 says,

> *"Trust in the Lord with all your heart, on your own intelligence rely not; in all your ways be mindful of him, and he will make straight your paths." (NAB)*

I thank God for knowing and being patient with his daughter. I have always been thickheaded about figuring things out, thank God that He makes things plain for me. It was as if I was on a journey and I had no clue about, nor control over where the road was leading me. My mind chose crisis, a journey of danger.

My mom sat with me in the hospital prep room she was saying the Rosary and reassuring me that all would be well but she also noticed how nonchalant I was. She did not ask me any questions she just gave me curious glances. Prior to surgery I went to the bathroom and coughed up everything I could. I had to go into surgery minus phlegm and chest rattle so they would not cancel the procedure. Fibroid Tumors each the size of lemons had attacked my womb. My stomach had swollen and I was tired most times. The surgery is supposed to lighten the load that I felt in my lower region but I knew it would not lighten the heaviness in my heart.

The nurse came for me and walked me to the operating room on the way she wrapped me in a white blanket so that I would not be cold. Now, maybe it's just me, but anyone who can walk into surgery does not need surgery of this magnitude. I walked beside the nurse with a gait that seemed more like we were going to Wendy's for a burger instead of an operating room. My nerves caught up with me when I entered the operating room. The lights were bright, my young female doctor had jazz playing in the background. There was a diverse surgical team preparing the instruments that would play healing rhythms to the tune of my illness. Some would say that my illness stemmed from my years of sinning. This would not surprise me, but God has a way of allowing things to unfold for His grand purpose.

The surgical team included white males and females, an African-American male his surgical cap was Kinte-colored, the Anestisologist was Asian. This was a view of the world that God was looking for, a diverse world coming together—working together to blend—to infuse—healing rhythms, rhythms of love. Suddenly an African American female nurse stood in front of me. Her eyes were full of a peace that I had never seen. The eyes—the peace—consumed me, drew me in close and as if whispering, she said, *"Honey, it's going to be alright. You are going to move to the table and lay down."* I could hear nothing but her voice. The jazz music disappeared, I could see nothing but her eyes and a bright light that surrounded us. *"It will be fine. You will be fine and it will be over soon."*

Then she left. The room suddenly came back into focus again. It seemed like a Jekyl Island moment all over again. I looked at the team they were all smiling in their preparation. I looked down at myself and saw how the blanket was draped over one of my shoulders and wrapped around my middle, hanging to the floor. I looked like a black Jesus especially with my full locs hanging about my shoulders. I looked at the operating table that was made out of wood not only that it was in the shape of a cross. ***Oh Snap!*** In my nervousness I chuckled and I looked up to the ceiling and said aloud, *"Ok God very funny! You are good!"* I thought, what a way to go just like Jesus, crucifixion and all! I actually got excited about God taking me from this life. He was taking me from this life alright, taking me into a new life, making me into a new creature. My mind's idea of a crisis was actually becoming an opportunity for salvation.

One of the most powerful lessons that I learned and quickly forgot at this point in my journey from another mentor/father, George Augustus Stallings, Jr., was that God does not take us from this life, sin in the world takes us from this world. *"Therefore, just as through one person sin entered the world, and through sin, death, and thus death came to all, inasmuch as all sinned." (Romans 5:12 NAB)*

The nurse that walked me into the operating room said, *"Well, go on get up on the table."* I remember cracking a joke . . . *"You expect my hips to fit on that table?"* I was the only one finding humor in that moment. I climbed on the table, laid down, and stretched my arms wide. I was asleep before I knew it. Suddenly, my eyes "bugged" open they felt like they were bulging out of my head and my head was extended back. I remember screaming in my mind, ***"JESUS!"*** I saw a bright lamplight shinning in my face and my Asian Anestheologist was rubbing my face and saying, *"We got you sweetheart, we got you, you're ok, we just had to check something out."* Even in his loud proclamation he could not drown out the voice in my mind still screaming, **"JESUS!"** What happened? They heard a rattle in my throat. They did not say but I think they thought that I was dying; but far from it, I was being made over, I was being born again. During the surgery I had a "sabachthani" experience. My soul cried out at the darkest hour of my crucifixion . . . I was letting go of the old man and my being was taking on the new man.

After the excitement I went to sleep again. When I awoke I heard my son say, *"See grandma, I told you ma would be fine."* I saw my mother's face. I love the caring look that can be found in a loving mother's eyes. I smiled at her and nodded back into a dreamless sleep.

After being released from the hospital—the place where sleep is limited because of the poking and prodding done hour after hour I spent three weeks in my upper room, my bedroom, my haven of peace, where I was not experiencing peace. I felt uneasy, confused, and lonely yet I knew I was not alone. I just could not understand what God wanted from me. This was the last time my mother waited on me—served me. It was not easy for her to climb the steps to bring me my meals, but she would also come up to see if I was ok. *"Wanda, how do you feel?" "Wanda, are you hungry?" "Wanda do you need anything?"* My mom taught me hospitality—she taught me what the Lord meant by your "reasonable service" and I have never and will never forget what it means to serve. It means providing comfort, going out of your way to nourish, also the need to speak a kind word. I know that to give your reasonable service is also a form of healing. I am so grateful for this particular memory of my mother because soon after the tables turned.

I was glad that prior to surgery I painted my room the color of the sun—a bright yellow—so that everyday for three weeks I could awaken in the light. I was missing church services. I missed my Imani Temple family. One of the Eucharistic Ministers came by to pray with me and give me Communion *(Thanks Queen Iris*). We talked about the greatness of God, I spoke about God wanting me—urging me—to do something but I did not know what. We prayed and talked and laughed once again I was served, nurtured, and healed. I found myself journaling more. I was driven to write poetry, it was my last book of poetry entitled, "Woven Baskets on the Baobab Tree." The book of poems was an abstract journey of my life from birth to womanhood as I sought to help the world. The words speak to my drowning in a sea of the world's hatred and pain, when suddenly I was assisted by Kelpie, a Native spirit in the form of a horse that either causes drowning or saves one from drowning. Kelpie was saving me with the help of my muses sent by Comfort spirit. My baskets were full of life experiences and now Comfort spirit called me back to Bantu Mountain where I could be at peace again. Sometimes poetry can be too deep for mainstream society to appreciate. But I self-published this book any way and sold a hundred copies or more. But the book was more for my clarity. God wanted me to see from whence I had come before I could be taken to the next level.

The next level of clarity came one Sunday morning. I turned on my BET (Black Entertainment Television) ministers. Bishop T.D. Jakes was on. He is one of the most fiery country preachers on the planet and God seemed to use him to dialogue truth just for and to me this particular Sunday. There are times when T.D. is preachin' his heart out and I cannot hear him. This is when I know the message is not mine. But this particular Sunday, on this great gettin' up morning Bishop Jakes might as well stuck his head out of the television screen and said, ***"HEY WANDA! GOD'S GOT A MESSAGE FOR YOU!"*** I was laying on the bed feeling sluggish and melancholy when all of a sudden I heard, "God is calling you . . . ." I sat upright in my bed. *"I bet you don't know why all your friends have left you! One by one they all walked away. God has something for you to do."* I stood up on my feet and began shouting and doing a holy dance. It is hard to keep still when God is standing by. The presence of the Lord was there in my room in my sanctuary, in my television. The message—the entire sermon—was mine. I was in shock . . . God really is direct when He wants your attention. Oh yes, God had my attention. Bishop Jakes kept saying, "*God is calling you!*" I sat down slowly on the foot of my bed, dazed yet knowing that God was Calling me.

Have you ever known something but because of your past indiscretions, your easy lifestyle, you thought, *"God could not possibly want me."* I thought, *"Who am I that I could be beneficial to God?"* I went from *"Why me?"* to absolute fear and shame.

A Little Voice

"Although the Lord gives you the bread of adversity and the water of affliction, your teachers will be hidden no more; with your own eyes you will see them. Whether you turn to the right or to the left, your ears will hear a voice behind you, saying, 'This is the way; walk in it.' Then you will defile your idols overlaid with silver and your images covered with gold; you will throw them away like a menstrual cloth and say to them, 'Away with you!'"

—(Isaiah 30: 20-22 NIV)

After Bishop T. D. Jakes stuck his head through my television to deliver the message that God was calling me. I decided that I needed more concrete proof. I did not mean to be difficult, obstinate, or disrespectful but I wanted to be sure that God was the author of the message and not my painkillers. Over a period of seven or eight days the events of my life were biblical to say the least, but God knows me and God knew that He could leave no doubt in my mind.

God did for me what He did for Samuel he gave me a revelation. I was given a revelation. Samuel's mother promised him to the Lord for as long as he lived. Samuel grew up in the service of the Lord. While he ministered under Eli the Priest, Samuel heard a voice, not once, but three times his name was called but Samuel did not answer appropriately until the fourth time his name was called. Each time he heard his name he thought that Eli was calling out to him. Scripture says that Samuel was not familiar with the Lord. Samuel (at Eli's suggestion) finally addressed God, *"Speak for your servant is listening."* Samuel was acknowledged as a Prophet. The Lord stayed with Samuel and did not allow his words to be without power. *(See 1 Samuel Chapter 3)*

I am not claiming to be a Prophet but I know, as God is my witness that I, too, was being Called and all I needed was three times to answer correctly. I was laying on my bed writing in my journal and I heard, "Wanda." It was a soft voice but very clear. I remember in the Bible God said, *"The Lord said, "Go out and stand on the mountain in the presence of the Lord, for the Lord is about to pass by. Then a great and powerful wind tore the mountains apart and shattered the rocks before the Lord, but the Lord was not in the wind. After the wind there was an earthquake, but the Lord was not in the earthquake. After the earthquake came a fire, but the Lord was not in the fire. And after the fire came a gentle whisper." (1 Kings 19:11-12)* I thought it was mama calling me, but she knew I couldn't come down the steps and how could her voice carry from the dining room up the stairs and be so quiet, yet clear? I answered anyway, "Maam!" "I didn't call you Wanda." I went and laid back down. In another day or two I heard, **"Wanda!"** This time the voice was a little louder and I heard it in the doorway of my bedroom. I turned to look at the doorway, but did not see anyone standing there. I knew mama was downstairs looking at her soap operas, but I got up anyway and stood at the top of the staircase, "MAAM!!" I knew she did not call me, but maybe . . . I had to justify the voice. *"Wanda! What's wrong with you? I didn't call you! You hearing things?"* I said to myself, *"Well, I might be."* People just don't hear voices as a normal occurrence. I went back into my room and sat down on the foot of my bed and spoke aloud, *"Why me?"* I knew what I had to say when the voice called my name again.

"A person or agency by which the thought, wish, or purpose of another is expressed." This is how the Funk & Wagnall's Dictionary defines "voice." To hear a voice a voice without physical presence is Biblical to say the least. In the Old Testament Adam and Even heard God's voice all the time. Moses heard God's voice on top of the Mountain called Horeb. God talked to Noah and his sons saying, *"I now establish my covenant with you and with your descendants after you . . ." (Genesis 9: 8-9 NIV)* In the New Testament God sent angels as messengers to speak on His behalf. *". . . An angel of the Lord appeared to him in a dream and said, 'Joseph son of David, do not be afraid to take Mary home as your wife . . ." (Matthew 1:20 NIV)* The formless, in this case also sexless, uttering sound was a spirit. When I heard "the voice" I did not know what to think, things like this just did not happen in this day and age.

I was coming up on the end of my three-week sabbatical and I was almost home free, no more voices. I had begun going downstairs for my meals and mom was glad. She took me to my follow-up doctors appointment where I got a clean bill of health. I felt like a new woman and I was excited about my third trip. I was about to see one of those friends that disappeared and I always wanted to see Seattle because my brother lived there for years and often spoke of its beauty. I saw pictures of the woods, the mountains *(Ahhh, mountains),* the water, and the different islands. I was ready for a change of scene. Oh yeah, I was having a good day, I was experiencing a balance of joy and peace. The next day I spent time in my room getting my outfits lined up for going back to work. I laid down for a wonderful nights sleep, another day gone by and no voice. It was mid-day the next day and I was lounging on my bed looking out the window at the sun, the birds flying by with an azure blue sky for a backdrop. It was so quiet and still, no music and no television. I wanted to soak up all the peace and quiet that I could because it would be gone soon. Soon I would return to the hustle and bustle of work life. The world suffers from an over consumption of events, a multitude of sounds, and non-stop confusion. We never take time to be still, quiet, void of nonsense. How can we ever know ourselves if we constantly fill ourselves with other people's thoughts, plans, and ideas of what we need to do next? I was embracing God, praying to God, and knowing that I was a good woman who had come a long way. I had dreams of doing great things for the world—for God's people. As a trainer, as a poet, I wanted to guide people to their higher purpose. I was thinking happy, productive, healing thoughts my toes curled in joy and I had a glint of a smile in my eyes. I was glad to be alive. No more drama for my mama then there it was . . . **"Wanda."**

Seattle Makes Three

I was Called. It wasn't just any Call. God took the time to come into my room and sit down on my bed (so to speak) and I knew I had to put the collar on.

Two mountains and a voice and I still felt not the least bit confident about what was happening. *"God, your daughter is thick, are you sure you want me? God there are some people out there better than me who could do so much better than I."* I know that I frustrated my God but I am grateful that He is patient with His daughter and God never gives up on us don'cha know especially when He sees that you are seeking His goodness and love. We, to often, give up on ourselves but Elohim, Adonai, El Elyon, God never leaves us or forsakes us. I am a witness! Can I get a witness?!

I went to Karibu Bookstore looking for books that dealt with the Call in this day and age. I found a book entitled, *"God's Yes Was Louder Than My No: Rethinking the African American Call to Ministry"* by William H. Myers. I read this book in amazement because God did the same thing for others. Men and women heard a voice, saw a sign, and other acts and wonders that I felt that they too felt were only for biblical times. God is endless and God's mission is likewise endless, consistent, and true. Why wouldn't He do for us what He did for our fore parents? He wants all his babies to return to Him using His Son as an example of how to live, move, and have our being. There are some of us, not special, not "holier than thou" just ordinary people that God chooses to stand before his people with all their experiences, pain, hardships, and risqué living to deliver His Word, His warnings, His love aligned with a testimony of how they got over. WOE! What a responsibility! I had been shaped and molded by God to be one of these ordinary people. All this so that He would be glorified, so that people who hear will believe that God is a Wonder-Working God. And He was not finished taking me through the journey.

My bags were packed and I was ready to take the trip of a lifetime. Seattle here I come! The flight was a long one and I tried to break my own record for sleeping. A half-hour from landing I woke up and stretched. I was grateful for the empty middle seat. As a full-figured woman airplane seating is a punishment. I always ask for a window seat and I usually push back the armrest to allow my hips even more comfort. ***"Lord! We are still in the air."*** I felt like I had been sleeping for two days! Did I mention that I had occasional panic attacks? It began in the last half hour of the flight. I began breathing heavy, sweat beads formed on my head, and I felt like I was suffocating. I learned how to work through the attacks by changing my thoughts. I shifted in my seat so much along with the pained look on my face that I made the man on the aisle seat very nervous. He kept giving me a look of don't you try it. The more I shifted in my seat the more he shifted in his seat. I closed my eyes and began thinking of God, Jesus, "Lord! HELP ME!" Then the "DING!" and another kind of voice, another wonderful voice said, *"Prepare for landing." "THANK YOU GOD!"* I released a slow breath and relaxed.

At last I was walking through Seattle's Sea Tac Airport toward the luggage terminal. I pulled my bag behind me and walked toward the car rental desk. I was always nervous about driving in a strange place on a strange highway, any highway for that matter, but I took a deep breath and away I went. It was a beautiful clear day. The highway roads were clean and smooth. The traffic was heavy all the way into downtown Seattle. Next to Philadelphia and New York downtown Seattle is the tightest little city I had ever seen with cobblestone streets and trolley tracks. I drove to meet the ferry that would travel over the calming Puget Sound toward the Olympic Islands. The cars lined up and we drove our cars onto the ferry. I was like a little kid walking into her very own toy store. I pulled up close on the car in front of me, put my car in park, turned off the engine, and sat there. People were existing their cars and walking with a fury toward the stairs. *"Ok, I want to see what is up there too!"* I got out of the car slowly as the ferry moved slowly through the water. The houses along the shore were beautiful, like something out of a picture book or a movie about the rich and the richer. I climbed the stairs and saw that the view off the side expanded to an even better view of the water and the houses, it was exquisite! The next deck had high back booths to sit in and there was also a place to buy food and drink. I did not care about the food, I was being fed by the wonders of God. I remember telling God that He was a genius, an artist, and a Magnificent Wonder! I was just as relaxed as I had been in Palm Springs after Miko's massage.

The ferry pulled up to dry land and people scurried back to their cars and I followed the pack. Did you take any pictures? You bet I did! I brought at least three throwaway cameras with me. I drove off the ferry and headed for the resort location. I drove up and down hills, over bridges, around bends. Trees, trees, trees as far as the eye could see and when there was a clearing I could see mountains in the distance I was at peace with a lightness in my heart. I pulled into the resort and the beauty continued. I registered at the desk and drove to my room. I could have used a better view but it did not matter. I could open my door, walk down the steps, walk along the stone path, and there before me was the most beautiful view of the crisp waters of Puget Sound. Our God is a Mighty God!

The next morning I put on the blue business suit and hoisted my locs on top of my head for the conservative look. I was ready to stand and deliver my presentation. I walked into the conference room during a break and sized up the group. My mentor came over and greeted me with joy. He brought me to this wonderful place to present a session on individual development planning to his division employees. I did what God blessed me to do and I must have done well because on the next break people came over to thank me, to give me their experiences, to tell me who I reminded them of, and to ask me business as well as personal questions. After my session we had a western bar-b-que that was quite tasty.

I thought I would hang around and listen to the next presenter but my mentor wanted to take his daughters and I to a place he had heard about called, "Hurricane Ridge." I agreed and went back to my room to change. We pulled out, stopped at the local food mart for junk food and we drove on. I knew we were in Native country. On the way to the resort I saw a Totem by the side of the road, I could also feel the spirit—the energy—of the ancestors. I was quiet through most of the journey then we pulled up to a ranger's station. I looked out the window and looked up and could not see the tops of the trees. I thought, these are some old girls. I always equate trees to being strong women, they are deeply rooted in the earth to provide shelter and protection for whoever is in need.

The park ranger told us to go straight ahead. We thought that we were going through a straight path of woods for a while later seeing some type of rock formation. We were not ready for what we were about to see. I was not ready for what I was about to see. We drove into a clearing and moved forward to a two-lane road, one lane for cars going up and another lane for the cars coming down. We went up and around, up and around, up and up. On the passenger side there was a rock wall that climbed to the sky. On the driver's side there was the wide-open spaces and no railing to keep you from soaring off the side of the road, which looked like a drop that had no end. As we drove up around this massive rock we began to see the tops of trees. It took one hour of rising road before we reached our destination. We got out of the van and I could not believe where I was.

I had gone from the base of a mountain to seeing a mountain at a distance, and now I was standing on top of a mountain. When God desires to make a statement He delivers the Gettysburg Address. There was grassy land, rolling hills, with a curved walkway up the middle. To the right there was a luscious forest. Deer either walked freely around us or lounged on the grass. There was a sign on the edge of the grass near the walkway that warned humans to stay off the grass because it belonged to the deer. We stay on the concrete and they went wherever they felt like going. My brother-friend's daughters were so excited because they never saw snow before and along the ridge of the mountain was snow . . . I was on a snow-capped mountain. The girls took off running and giggling toward the snow. All I could do was stand in the middle of the walkway and stare at God's portrait of blue sky, tall trees, and in the distance the clouds in the sky became part of the mountaintops. My eyes teared up at the courtly, the miraculous, the incomprehensible view bestowed upon me. A lady was sidling past me on the walkway, *"Awesome isn't it?"* I looked away from my portrait for a second or two and said, *"Oh yes, it is, it really is."* I was mesmerized.

My brother-friend walked up behind me and softly said, *"You seem to have a friend." "What? Where?"* He said, *"Beside you."* I looked down and a deer was standing right beside me and then another was walking over to me. When you acknowledge God in your whole being animals are aware, sometimes more than people, of His presence as well and you all become one with God. Moses was drawn to the mountain, Jesus prayed up on the mountain, Dr. Martin Luther King, Jr., in his famous speech said metaphysically that he had been to the mountaintop. I was taken to the top of the mountain and my soul rejoiced!

First time in Seattle, first ferry ride, my room was by the water, and my presentation was successful, but the most unfathomable experience of the entire trip was standing on the top of a snow-capped mountain. *"How beautiful upon the mountains are the feet of (her) who brings glad tidings, announcing peace, bearing good news, announcing salvation and saying to Zion, 'Your God is King!'" (Isaiah 52:7 NAB)* God was telling me my feet were beautiful and I had to bring the good news, I had to share the news of redemption, salvation, and peace. I knew, I at last knew, that I had received the "Call" not from a man—not from a woman—from God, the God of Abraham, Isaac, and Jacob who took time to take me through a communicative journey of signs and wonders. God gave me this third mountain as a gift of His love. I accepted my Call to ordained ministry.

> *"Awake, awake O Zion clothe yourself with strength. Put on your garments of splendor, O Jerusalem, the holy city. The uncircumcised and defiled will not enter you again. Shake off your dust; rise up, sit enthroned, O Jerusalem. Free yourself from the chains on your neck. O captive Daughter of Zion."*
>
> *—(Isaiah 52: 1-2 NIV)*

I was set free, cleansed of the world, and my purpose was revealed. I awakened to the fact that I was already clothed with strength and splendor, I just needed it to come forth. When you see the face of God in God's wonders, when you are in the presence of the Lord, you will bow down, and you will serve. I was born to be a minister of God. Oh! Wait. I belong to the African-American Catholic Congregation . . . CATHOLIC. Oh man, I was going to be a Catholic Priest. Oh my! It was clear God made the Call and I answered God not a man or a man's laws but God's!

Some time after I returned home God sent someone to me to solidify the Call. After a church function I took one of the choir members home. I have always admired this lady and she reminds me of me because she rather observe than talk a lot (Well, I use to be quiet.) When I pulled up in front of her home she said, *"Come in."* I really did not feel like it I was tired and wanted to go home but she insisted and it is rare that this woman asked for anything. I went in and she said that she did not know why but she had something to show me. She put a tape into the VCR. She said that she loved Bishop T.D. Jakes and I said so do I. The next thing that I heard . . . *"God is calling you . . . I bet you don't know why all your friends have left you! One by one they all walked away. God has something for you to do."* Got'cha God! Through my tears I said, Yes Lord! Thank you Sister Karen Moore for you, too, heard the voice of God.

Motivators, Inspirationalists, and Teachers: You Have My Undying Love

There were those who belong to the early years of Imani Temple before Imani Temple was Imani Temple, those who came together, developed, and helped to build the foundation. I want to celebrate the professors, scholars, historians, analyst, preachers, prophets, yes revolutionaries, all those who researched and wrote the Imani Temple holy documents, those who gave reassuring words to a man who had his doubts, a man who received death threats, a man who spent late night hours with these professors, preachers, and prophets, those who are now completely spirit constructed an institution.

Bishop Glenn Vincent Jeanmarie
Father Charles Stephney
Father Paul Anthony Dillard, Jr.

There was a Marist Brother who was my teacher early in my formation, Brother Cyprian Lamar Rowe. He joined Imani Temple and became a Priest and then a Bishop. His favorite saying is *"Everything is a Grace."* He believed in reaching out to the less fortunate and he loves cats. Bishop Rowe, I love you.

Finally, another Brother who was in my life briefly, but who made a monumental impact in my life and he is now an Ancestor, Brother Joseph Hagar.

He taught me that even a free spirit, a revolutionary, has to be obedient and disciplined. Brother Hager made the Word of God breathe. We had wonderful real life conversations and I miss him dragging out . . . *"Honey!"*

These men knew/know the importance of the sacred feminine balancing out the spirituality. They let me know that my place, my position, was vital to the African-American Catholic Congregation as well as the entire Christian community before I even received the Call. They always spoke of Liberation Theology, which simply put addresses the struggles of the poor and oppressed and the necessity of the church to address their needs in the context of God's word. Liberating the people just as Moses liberated the Israelites from Egypt. I embrace Liberation Theology.

When I think of liberation and balance I think of women ministers who have touched my life. I know empowered daughters of God, preachin' and teachin' women anointed and appointed by God. Revered Jackie Nelson who has been a sister in the gap for me. When I called she always answered. Another fearsome sister warrior is Bishop Vashti McKenzie. I never met her but I know when I see and hear God's power and He rules and reigns in this sister Bishop. Another sister Reverend who has put me in touch with other powerful sisters, Reverend Addie Robb, Director of Women Uplifting Women Ministries. She has been a soldier for Christ for quite some time. She helps the elderly and her soul desire is to spread the word of God. Though a warrior she is also a peacekeeper who keeps me focused. I have traveled around the Washington, D.C. area to various churches preaching with her and other preaching women and our spirits are connected forever. Lastly, there is a woman called to be of a different cloth, a nun named Sister Rosetta Brown, a revolutionary for children. She taught me how to see as well as praise God in the face of the enemy.

Thank you Sister warriors of God! Thank you all for listening to the voice of God for yourselves and for me.

Denomination Did Not Call You

1 Corinthians 3:19 states, *"For the wisdom of this world is foolishness in God's sight. As it is written: 'He catches the wise in their craftiness.'"* God gave man the wisdom to create various avenues with which to connect with Him based on the diverse needs of His people.

The secular meaning for denomination is the act of calling by name a class, group, things, or a people. (Funk & Wagnall's Standard Desk Dictionary, Vol. 1, 1984) God gave Adam the honor of naming all the creatures of the earth and man has continued this Adam legacy throughout the years. Leo Pfeffer once said, ". . . if you believe in it, it is a religion or perhaps 'the' religion; and if you do not care one way or another about it, it is a sect; but if you fear and hate it, it is a cult." Mr. Pfeffer was not far off. The definition of denomination that most people recognize is an established religious group, which has been in existence for many years with national and international membership. *(www.relioustolerance.org)*

What does denomination have to do with my Call story? A lot! My denomination is the African-American Catholic Congregation (AACC) considered to be a "sect" (has been called a cult) because it is an offshoot of an established religion, the Roman Catholic Church. We broke away July 2, 1989. I love my denomination because as I said before it is a blend of my mother and father. The AACC is not better than or less than any other Christian denomination; it is, like other Christian religions, another venue by which to worship God in spirit and in truth. I counted 180 denominations and I know there are many more. All of these denominations profess to love God, Jesus, and the Holy Ghost/Spirit. If this is so, then why do denominations look down their noses at other denominations? Where is Christ in all of that? Where is the Spirit of God in our judgments?

Man and woman's ego has blown denominations and their purpose for being way out of control. In other words, man and woman are becoming full of their own wisdom instead of relying on God's wisdom. A speaker came to my Trinity College class on African-American Religious Experience. The professor invited speakers from different denominations to talk about their religious practices. One woman from the Baptist church made the statement that *"You Catholics say the Lord's Prayer incorrectly."* We were aghast! Someone asked her, *"Just what way is the right way?"* She pointed out the version that is in the Bible as the accurate way. If that is the way her denomination says the Lord's Prayer that's great, but it is also fine if another denomination says it differently. Let me tell you what counts the most. As a Christian, if you serve God, the Father of Abraham, Isaac, and Jacob, if you know Jesus as your Lord and Savior, and you live, move, and have your being under the Holy Spirit then why haggle over how the Lord's Prayer is said. Where is your heart when you pray is what I want to know? God wants to not only know where is your heart when you pray but do you love Him with your whole heart, your whole soul and with your whole mind and do you love your neighbor as yourself. Does your denomination praise God? Does your denomination teach the teachings of Christ? That's what is important.

It is vitally important that when you receive the Call that you know denomination is not the big picture but whether you were really Called to ordained ministry. Some people are Called to serve as Lectors, Ushers, or Evangelist. *"There are different kinds of spiritual gifts but the same Spirit; there are different forms of service but the same Lord; there are different workings but the same God who produces all of them in everyone . . . . To one is given through the Spirit the expression of wisdom; to another the expression of knowledge, according to the same Spirit; to another faith by the same Spirit; to another gifts of healing by the one Spirit; to another mighty deeds; to another prophecy; to another discernment of spirits; to another varieties of tongues; to another interpretation of tongues. But one and the same Spirit produces all of these, distributing them individually to each person as he wishes." (1 Corinthians 12:4-6, 8-11)* Ask God for clarity about what He is calling you to do and be. If the AACC became non-existent I would still be a priest serving God in spirit and in truth wherever I am.

How did I know I was being Called? It was the chain of events and the events themselves. God knew I was ready to listen to His voice because He set everything in motion. I have been working in the church all my life, first the Roman Catholic Church then in the African-American Catholic Congregation. I sang in the choir in the Roman Catholic Church in the AACC I served as a Lector and later became the National Head of the Lector Ministry. I started the Sisters of Imani. I assisted with our New Members Ministry and the Kwanzaa Ministry. At the age of 40 I danced on stage at the Anniversary of the African Heritage Dancers and Drummers who are also a Ministry at Imani Temple. God was moving in an astronomical way in my life. I asked God where did He want me to be now. I was not going to assume God wanted me to stay at Imani Temple even though when I accepted the Call my first thought was, *"I am going to be a Priest."* I still needed to be good and clear about where I was suppose to be. God has made three things very clear to me:

1. I answer to God.
2. God said, "Preach to and Teach them and I will do the rest."
3. Stay at Imani for the people.

So it is, I am a Catholic Priest. I am not caught up in denomination even though I have been a Catholic since infancy, but I am overwhelmed by the power of God in Catholicism and I, as His child, am an obedient servant to His will and His way. Since I happen to be under the AACC I also am obedient to the shepherd of this denomination.

I just want you to know that the denomination is where you serve but God Calls you. Know God for your self, study the Word of God as well as other spiritual, theological, and the various reference materials to show thyself approved. As a matter of fact, when you do not understand something ask God for the answer and He will provide the answer through a book, a magazine, or a person. Do not lock God in a denominational box be willing to know Him beyond the boundaries of man and woman's preferred views.

Today, If You Hear His Voice . . .

God cannot use a hardened heart but God can surely soften it. If you have distractions in your life that prevent you from hearing the voice of God, God will remove those distractions one-by-one. Then when you hear His voice, trust Him. God will not tell you to do anything harmful to yourself or others. His voice is a voice of love.

September 8, 2001, I was ordained to the Diaconate and on July 14, 2002, nine months later, I became a Priest. God carried me in the womb where I read theology books and articles. I ingested Metaphysical teachings. I learned about the various parts of the Mass. I went to Bishop Rowe's house and sat in the kitchen with other candidates hearing about liberation theology. Nine months . . . the number nine is a product of (3x3x3) which means Divine completeness and finality of judgment. Let's look back, three friends were temporarily removed from my life, I was given three mountain views, and a voice, God's voice, Called me three times. God gave birth to a new creation. I was made complete to do His work.

Roman Catholic Priests believe that women in no way, shape, or form can be Priests. There are Baptist ministers that use the Scriptures taken from Matthew 10: 1-4 or Mark 3: 13-19, or Luke 6: 12-16 that talk about the twelve MEN, not women, that were called to follow Jesus. But they neglect other Scriptures, *"When he had risen, early on the first day of the week, he appeared first to Mary Magdalene out of whom he had driven seven demons. She went and told his companions who were mourning and weeping. When they heard that he was alive and had been seen by her, they did not believe."—Mark 16:9-11*

In the Gospel of Luke, Mary was not alone Joanna and Mary, the mother of James, were also there. Jesus appeared to those who were working out of faith and not fear. Am I saying that men are afraid? No, but the women were not in the upper room wondering if they were going to be linked with the Savior. Let's be real, the men would have had the women with them but it is possible that they assumed the women were safe because they could not possibly have anything of substance to do with the Jesus Movement. It is unfortunate that so many men have tainted the Spirit of the Gospel, thus they have tainted themselves and others. During my formation as Deacon I was blessed to be Pastor of one of our outpost Temples where I learned patience, endurance, and my favorite quality, humility. The number of congregants grew and so did the Tithes and offerings. My mom, who once thought that I was going to hell in a hand basket when I joined Imani Temple, was about to join before she got too ill to come out. Then I was promoted to Assistant Dean at the Mother Cathedral on Capitol Hill. I bet you are wondering how could Archbishop Stallings move her so quickly. You are not alone; there were clergy and congregants who wondered about the same thing. Archbishop never addressed my progression and he never should. I know and he knows that God elevates and Archbishop had no choice but to do what he did if he wanted to be obedient to the will of God.

The most important qualities that a minister should posses are obedience, patience, and humility. Yes, it would be the hardest of qualities to obtain, but I dare you to ask God to increase these qualities inside of you . . . "God, give me patience." Let me tell you how it worked when I asked for patience. Any situation or person that tried my patience confronted me so that I had to be patient as well as humble. I was made to push out qualities that lay dormant inside of me. When God reshapes you, breaks you, and makes you new it's like being a little child again trying to learn new social skills. In this new body highlighted by a new spirit you cannot cuss folk out. You cannot roll your eyes, or point your fingers. You cannot hold grudges or threaten to punch people in the face. How hard is this?! Well, I found out that even as a new creature it was hard because I still had moments. I twitch a lot, close my eyes a lot and take many many deep breaths. You see, I often return to my youth, lil' Wanda Brown, who spoke very little but observed much. She, I, spoke only when I had a question or when I needed to make an observation and wanted people to know that I knew something about what was going on or what they were talking about which usually made them get quiet around me. This is my father, Augustus King Brown coming out in me. This is how I struggle to keep my self from saying hurtful things or judgmental statements. I got through some bumpy times as a Pastor when my congregants decided that they wanted to tell me what to preach about, along with other criticism's they could dole out in order to make me a better Deacon/Pastor. I became better, but not for the reasons that they think. I increased not only in patience and humility but also in compassion for a people who showed me love the best way that they knew how.

I have seen my brother clergy struggle through humility and ego. A huge ego can kill you. One of my clergy brother's, Father Bayo, says that all ego means is "Edging God Out," so very true! Women as well as men struggle with ego. But women it is important for you to know and to remind your brothers that because you are a woman humility in you does not mean "easy prey," "soft touch," or "push over." To be humble means that you, the "I" the "man-self" decreases so that God increases. When someone steps up to the ATM line you turn to position yourself behind the next person and the person who walked up behind you steps in front of you . . . what do you do when they turn to look at you to say, *"I was in line before you."* You say nothing. Let's not forget the person standing in a "15 items" line with 30 items in the cart and even though they are in front of you in line, sometimes it is easier to stay peaceful, to stay quiet. These moments are not worth the energy and you know you should praise God, you can stand, you can walk, at least you can get groceries, and you can get money when you need to. And then there is the minister who gets less attention than the other ministers so he or she asserts themselves into situations or discussions just to be acknowledged. It is about having a humble and loving attitude and posture, how you carry yourself and how you love God's people as you love yourself. It's not about what you can get but what you can give. The question that looms large within the Greatest Commandment is, do you love yourself? You cannot love others like yourself if you do not love yourself.

Even humble men and women can still be revolutionaries. There is nothing wrong with taking a platform against an injustice, Jesus did. Remember those Sadducees and Pharisees? Begin at *Matthew 23:16, "Woe to you, blind guides, who say, 'If one swears by the temple, it means nothing, but if one swears by the gold of the temple, one is obligated.' Blind fools, which is greater, the gold or the temple that made the gold sacred?"* Even Jesus had to call out foolishness every now and again.

I am a child of God, who happens to be an African-American woman, a revolutionary who was Called to be a Catholic Priest. No man, no woman, can take this from me. I wrote this book, told my story, to open up your consciousness (your sense of awareness, of knowing) to the truth. God loves working with, through, and in a people who by humbling themselves, leave Him room to make new changes, to bring about new growth, to impart new wisdom and revelations to all those who seek it.

Everyone's Call is different, yet there seems to be some similarities in the magnitude of the Call. Stop yourself from thinking that visions, voices, and manifestations are fake, phony, spooky, scary, or witchcraft; to think this is to think thoughts that oppose the Bible. *"After six days Jesus took Peter, James, and John his brother, and led them up a high mountain by themselves. And he was transfigured before them; his face shone like the sun and his clothes became white as light. And behold, Moses and Elijah appeared to them, conversing with him." (Matthew 17: 1-3 NAB)* We have to let go of Hollywood concepts, spiritually speaking, thoughts of a worldly nature, we are in the world but we came from God who is not of this world and likewise neither are we. God Calls us to do different things to His glory. Your call does not have to be ordained ministry. God can Call you to adopt a child, go back to college, start a neighborhood Bible Study, be an administrator in the church, get married, or sing in the church choir. Listen. Sit in quiet and listen to the voice of God, pray, ask for clarity, and then obey His voice.

Before my mother died she said, *"I know you want to do your ministry work."* She thought that she was holding me back but she was my ministry as well. I was responsible and called to be a caregiver and loyal daughter to my mother. Mama told me, *"Wanda you just take such good care of me. I don't know what I would do without you."* I don't know what I would have done without her! She was a blessing so was my dad. Mom was the woman who made me comfortable with all aspects of the living and the dead. She died March 11, 2003, and I have moved forward in my ministry work ever since knowing/remembering all that she taught me, embracing all the experiences, and all the highs and lows along the way. I will never forget this journey and those who were stepping stones toward the goal. I always believe that to be credible as a minister of God you have to:

1) Take care of your household and family within or you cannot take care of the church house. God gives us the small things to see if we can be responsible in those small things before He gives us something larger.
2) We have to forgive all those who have ever offended us in order to move forward in our lives and our ministry.
3) We must not ostracize any man, woman, or child. No matter what we have to love EVERYONE.
4) Stay humble because the ministry has very little to do with you and it solely has to do with God and God's people and your mandate to serve.

God used three mountains and a voice to get through to me. God also used some spirit angels along the way to guide my path. God will guide you too. If He brings you to it He will guide you through it. I pray let it be done for you according to your faith.

"At once [Jesus] spoke to them, 'Take courage, it is I; do not be afraid.' Peter said to him in reply, 'Lord if it is you, command me to come to you on the water.' He said, 'Come.' Peter got out of the boat and began to walk on the water toward Jesus." Matthew 14:29,

My Call is not your Call. God works with everyone right where they are in their lives. My mountain could be your ocean, or your tree.

You cannot tell everyone about your Call journey while you are in the midst of it. Yes, they might think you have left the planet. If you have God-fearing confidants who support you in your spirituality you might be able to confide in them about your journey. If you are not sure that you can it is better that you don't. While I was in the midst of the journey I told no one just like I usually do not tell people about the spirits that I see. Even the most God-grounded individual cannot always handle hearing that the spiritual realm lives and moves beside us.

In the midst of your Call, whatever that Call is, be still, be silent before the Lord so that you can hear His voice. I pray that you walk toward Jesus, walk like Jesus, listen to that quiet little voice, and do not be afraid. I pray . . .

Precious and Loving God anoint the person reading this book right now from the top of their head to the soles of their feet, from finger tip to finger tip in the Name of Jesus. Raise them in their purpose so that they can fulfill Your Holy Will for Your glory. Amen, Amen, and Amen!

God Loves you and so do I!

Edwards Brothers Malloy
Thorofare, NJ USA
April 16, 2014